The Book of Womanhood

The Book of Womanhood

Amy F. Davis Abdallah
foreword by Lisa Graham McMinn

CASCADE *Books* · Eugene, Oregon

Cascade Books
An Imprint of Wipf and Stock Publishers
199 W. 8th Ave., Suite 3
Eugene, OR 97401

ISBN 13: 978-1-4982-2134-4

www.wipfandstock.com

Cataloging-in-Publication data:

Davis Abdallah, Amy F.

xviii + 204 p.; 23 cm—Includes bibliographical references

The book of womanhood / Amy F. Davis Abdallah.

ISBN 13: 978-1-4982-2134-4

1. Women's spirituality. 2. Women and religion. 3. Title

BL458 .A230 2015

for the women

Table of Contents

List of Tables

Foreword

MY FATHER LIKED ADVENTURES. While I think he would have preferred more sons and fewer daughters (he got three daughters before getting his son), it meant we girls were drawn into his adventuring.

I'd like to think I was the most adventurous of us all.

Some of us climbed mountains with Dad, and I climbed the tree just beside the front porch and scrambled up on the rooftop to look at stars with him. We hiked together, and he tried to teach all of us how to properly catch and throw a football. Some of us kids tended wounded birds with him, and when it was his turn to preach, he took all of us to the Gospel Rescue Mission to eat dinner with the homeless people after the sermon.

This is not to ignore my mother's role in shaping me. It was less adventurous, but equally important. I joined her in the kitchen and acquired a love of baking and cooking, an altogether underappreciated way of being creative and offering a deeply nourishing kind of love. She taught me to knit, and tried to teach me to sew, and let me run off to play in the desert with my brother when I couldn't stand to sit another moment.

My parents made a strong woman out of me, teaching me it was okay to "buck the system," to go against the flow, to stand firm like Noah in an unfriendly, ungodly world. I did not appreciate a lot of this at the time. Especially not when Dad would compare our family to Noah's when he was denying yet another request to do something every other girl I knew was doing.

My father may have regretted imparting all that confidence and courage in later years. I told him once that the strength he thought I had taken too far (getting a PhD, pursuing a career that had me teaching men) came from the courage and fortitude he instilled when I was an impressionable daughter growing up in his home.

I count myself blessed, even though not completely untarnished by what was also a very strict and conservative upbringing. Not all girls grow up with parents that affirm them as capable, intelligent, creative beings with something worthwhile to contribute to the world. You'll discover that Amy Davis Abdallah, like I, has taught a good number of women who are unsure what it is supposed to mean to "be a woman." They lack the confidence that enables them to give and receive love from God, to accept and love themselves, to accept and love others, and to engage God's good creation in responsible and creative ways—all relationships that Amy dives into in this field guide exploration of the identity of women.

Even the most confident young women stumble. We live in a wonderfully diverse culture, and while there are many upsides to that, one downside is that it is full of mixed messages about what it means to be a woman, or a man for that matter. Except for a driver's license at sixteen and the right to drink at twenty-one, we don't have markers that help girls and boys transition from childhood to young adulthood to adulthood. Even with the stability of my childhood home I stumbled around a bit once I deviated from the path my parents expected me to tread.

I looked around for role models and too many of the strong women I saw at the time seemed either angry and/or overly focused on the privileges still denied them. I wanted to forge a way that empowered me, and later my daughters and female students, to transition into adulthood as women called by God to walk humbly in the light of God's love, partnering with men and other women in the pursuit of justice and mercy.

Amy has crafted an experience that attempts to do just that. *Woman* is a rite of passage of sorts that brings a group together to explore their identity as women and how that is fleshed out in various relationships. How much clearer such a journey is when some kind of shared rite of passage is woven into a culture's fabric! How much richer the experience is when shared with other sojourners, and applauded by onlookers who are invested in seeing the participants succeed!

I'd researched and written some about rites of passages, which later connected me to Amy. I learned of her interest in creating a rite of passage for women when she asked me to be on her dissertation committee, the dissertation itself an exploration of rites of passage. She took theological truths, historical traditions, and theoretical ideas, and applied them, creating a rite of passage for women at Nyack College, an experience that would strengthen their identity as women loved and gifted by God.

The book you hold in your hands is based on the findings from that dissertation and Amy's subsequent work writing about, developing, and implementing *Woman*. Amy developed a rite that fits our twenty-first-century Western evangelical culture, addressing the questions of our day, which in many ways are similar to questions of the past, but in significant ways are also different. Wisely, Amy doesn't prepare and send women off on solo journeys into the woods to hunt and kill a beast, and so to establish themselves as worthy and ready for womanhood. Rather she walks them through a course of study that builds on humanity's four classic relationships: with God, with ourselves, with others, and with creation. In those properly aligned relationships our identity as women grows stronger, as does our capacity to live well, to contribute wisely to the world, and to participate with God in making the world a light- and love-filled place.

Amy has been leading groups through the rite of passage at Nyack College for about four years now, though participants have not only been college-age women. While historically a rite of passage was linked to a particular time in an individual's life, this book is designed to come alongside women at any point from young adulthood onward, fostering a stronger sense of what it means to be women made in the image of God.

Enter the journey with enthusiasm—and with at least a friend or two—and enjoy the challenge of exploring the opportunities and responsibilities of being a woman loved by God, and called to love, and to pursue mercy and justice.

Lisa Graham McMinn, PhD
Professor of Sociology
George Fox University
Author of *Growing Strong Daughters*

Preface

WHEN I WAS ABOUT sixteen, a pastor told me to be less assertive and strong because otherwise I'd never find a husband. Mom says I came home saying I couldn't deny who I really was in order to please others.

But my husbandless twenties left me wondering about who I was. Not about whether I was assertive or strong, but about my identity as a woman. I had only understood womanhood in the roles of wife and mother, roles I did not have.

Herein, my journey to find what it means to be a Christian woman is found. There are bits and pieces of the stories that make my life and my womanhood—travel, study, teaching—and bits and pieces of my friends' and students' stories, too. Mostly, it's a guide that helps us understand ourselves as women, using the framework of relationship with God, self, others, and creation.

It's a flexible framework. Its purpose is to inspire you to think, not to tell you to change yourself to please others. In fact, as you read, I hope that you realize being a woman is simply figuring out how to fully be yourself, not fulfilling some kind of "womanly role."

May these pages help answer your identity questions.

May these pages encourage and empower you to fully be *yourself*.

May Holy Spirit fire restore the Divine Image in you, woman of God!

Acknowledgments

THIS BOOK IS ABOUT my journey, and like any trip, it's hard to remember all the sights that made it so beautiful and rich! Thus, though I will try here to remember the salient participants in my journey, without a doubt, many will be inadvertently left out. Yet, even to them, I am still grateful.

Gratefulness has been my most important spiritual discipline lately. It has led me from a life that saw only what needed fixing to a life that rejoices over what is already good. Gratefulness brings joy, and the people here have brought great joy and hope to my journey; their stories are included in the text.

I'm thankful for my early singular examples in Martha and Lorri. I remember Mr. Tanner for calling me beautiful, Gene for encouraging me to ask, Amal for showing me the meaning of hospitality, and Dad for teaching me how to use a car-owner's manual.

I'll never forget my hiking partner Michele, my financial advisor Theresa, and my healing friendships with Ken, Dave, and Steve. And though it was embarrassing at the time, I'm thankful that my grandfather watched *When Harry Met Sally* with me. My internship mentor, Don, and my professors Paul and Bryan made a significant positive impact on my life.

I'm blessed to share the journeys of the participants in *Woman* and the individual stories of Christina, Thressa, and Rachel. I offer thanks to those who've shared their journeys with me—to Lisa for decorating, Wanda for cooking, Mom for gardening, and Janice for being all-around amazing. The powerhouse leaders of *Woman* also deserve mention—Wanda, Wanda, and Christina. Thank you for believing in me and helping so many in our journeys of womanhood!

As for the nitty-gritty work of writing, I thank Maureen, Kim, and Julie, who helped with parts of the manuscript, and Valentina, who formatted the bibliography.

Those who've walked closest to me in my early journey are Mom, Dad, Sharon, and Brian—your influence and stories flow throughout this work! But the ones sharing my journey now are Ghiath and Jaohar, who inspire and empower me to be fully myself.

"Thanks" seems so insufficient, but even so, I offer it. Thanks for walking the journey with me so far. Thanks for walking into the future with me.

To God be the glory.

Introduction

IT IS A SPECIAL evening, one of my favorite evenings of the year. After months of preparation, we are about to initiate the third class of participants in the rite of passage called *Woman*. The atmosphere is perfect—candles are lit, gifts laid out, desserts visible, and alumnae are assisting. All the college student participants are in semiformal attire sitting somewhat nervously in a half circle, not quite sure what the evening will be like, since this is their first "initiation." Before beginning the initiation rite, I ask each of the women to share why they chose to invest themselves in this voluntary process that offers mostly intangible results and no academic credit. Many state that they were raised in a Christian subculture that implicitly (and sometimes explicitly) taught them that marriage made them a woman. They, however, are convinced that being a woman is not simply being married, and are participating in the rite of passage in order to find a framework that helps to define themselves as women, whether single or married, whether with children or without. I am invigorated, knowing that their life stories will be different from mine because of *Woman*.

I remember knowing two single women in the small-town upstate New York church we attended during my formative years. One was the divorced mother of my friend and the other was on her way to be a missionary. Almost all the others were married with children. My extended family all married young, most to high school or college sweethearts, and the women focused on their children. Predictably, then, my college hopes included meeting the man of my dreams, marrying soon after, and becoming an elementary school teacher who took time off for her children's early years and then spent summers with the kids when they started school. I simply thought that was what women did—women found their identity in the roles of wife and mother.

1

As with most of us, life did not happen quite the way I imagined it would when I was eighteen. I took the fact I did not marry (or have) a college sweetheart in stride, enjoying the freedom to travel to Asunción, Paraguay and to teach there, although I must admit my hopes were still similar to the college ones. I was part of the *jovenes* (youth) group at church—a group of teenagers and any others who were unmarried. After two years, I returned stateside, and my new teaching job brought me to a church in Pennsylvania that was similar to my earliest one. There, I often wondered why people thought I was still in college—it certainly wasn't my young fashion style since I was a dowdy schoolteacher whose drop-waist dresses functioned to free her to sit on the floor with the littlest students. Was I immature? Was it my marital state? I knew I was in the fourth year of my teaching career, but was I a woman or still just a girl?

My heart longed for international work, so I left my public school teaching career to pursue a seminary education, still with the hope that this new stage in life would provide me with what I had desired in college. But people do not blunderingly call seminary "cemetery" without cause. At graduation, I was no longer headed to full-time international work, and I was still alone, wondering where I fit, whether I was a girl or a woman, and what it meant to be a woman anyway.

I can picture the room that held my first forty-student college Bible class and I can still feel the jitters that I experienced most of that semester. I was a full-time college instructor, but as I looked out at the sea of young faces, I felt like I was one of them, often identifying more with them than with my married colleagues. I deeply knew, however, that I was an adult, not a college student, and a woman, not a girl. My identity as a woman had not been found in the roles of wife and mother, so I began a journey of naming myself "woman" and seeking to define that.

Though we've not grown up the same and our experiences profoundly differ, I find that many women still wonder about womanhood in a similar way, regardless of how their backgrounds defined womanhood. A woman may refer to a friend as "her girl," and may have only heard the term "woman" in a pejorative context. Media and society encourage her to find empowerment in a "Girls Gone Wild" or "Spring Break" rite of passage experience, and to allow her peers and the opposite sex to form her meaning and identity. The Christian church negates these ideas, but offers discipleship that is often one-dimensional teaching about following God's commands. She needs more than that. She needs to know what being a

Christian woman is and when and how she can become one. That's what I was searching for when I began to name myself "woman."

It was a significant step for me to stop referring to myself as a girl, whether out loud or in my head, but this journey of womanhood did not suddenly take all of my attention. Sure, being the only full-time female professor in the Bible and Christian ministry department made me consider gender questions, and they came up in classes, but the journey of womanhood did not suddenly become central to my life.

Seven years after that first college class I taught, however, my first dissertation topic gets rejected, and I need a new one. My advisor suggests that I review all my previous papers and projects to see if any still interest me, and my work on rites of passage for women stands out. As the dissertation project is approved and all the details fall into place, the journey of womanhood comes front and center. I want to know how others envision the passage from girl to woman and to analyze it ritually and theologically. *Woman,* Nyack's rite of passage, is the result of that research, and I now have a framework that encapsulates how I understand myself as a Christian woman.

Why a Rite of Passage?

Like many others, I began the journey to understand myself as a woman without a rite of passage. Rather than citing a distinct ritual, Christian women may narrate a series of several life experiences that catalyzed their transformation from girl to woman, while others may lament continuing confusion about womanhood. Still others may argue that becoming a woman is a daily, gradual occurrence that happens through gaining more responsibility at home or various "passage activities," like "beginning menstruation, getting a driver's license, reaching drinking age, graduating, moving away from the parental home, or earning an income."[1] These events are often unritualized and happen at different times for each person.

Without the presence of a rite of passage into adulthood, however, defining oneself as a woman is not only done at varying ages and degrees of maturity: it is also neglected, leaving the person who has adult responsibilities still feeling like a girl and unsure of her womanhood (like me).

Though many American Christians are suspicious of ritual and symbol, we return to them at the most important times of life. Students look

1. Grimes, *Deeply into the Bone,* 94.

forward to a graduation full of "pomp and circumstance," special symbolic clothing, "crossing the stage," and changing the tassel from right to left. Even the most nontraditional pastors celebrate a traditional wedding ritual where participants wear distinctive clothing, are physically given to one another, and adorn their left ring fingers with the symbols of that union. And when life has expired, we find comfort in a ritual that includes the biblical readings of future hope, the flowers and casket, and the line of cars with headlights on, journeying to the place of rest. These are not the "dead rituals" that provoke the ire of American Christians. No, they are meaning-ful ceremonies that accompany some of the most important rites of passage in life. In fact, "Although rituals tend to be conservative, that is, valuing the past and honoring tradition, rituals can also be innovative, that is, training their participants into a new way of thinking."[2]

In 1994, *The Encyclopedia of World Problems and Human Potential* cited the lack of rites of passage in global society as a problem that results in confusion regarding the marks of age-related social roles and the soci-etal requirements for those roles.[3] To mark passage to adulthood and adult social roles, some celebrate a *quinceañera* or a debutante ball, but most just float through this time as liminal, "betwixt and between," wondering who they are and where they fit into the unclear societal or Christian scheme. A rite of passage into Christian womanhood can clarify the Christian scheme and provide teaching and experiences that grow a Christian daughter by referring to her whole being—spiritual, psychological, social, sexual, intel-lectual, and emotional.[4]

Rites of Passage Basics

Arnold van Gennep coined the phrase "rite of passage" as a descriptor of his research into "coming-of-age" rituals in indigenous tribes at the turn of the twentieth century. At that time, it was typical to observe only male rituals as the archetype for both genders, and he found that the ones he observed had three stages: preliminal, liminal, and postliminal, or "rites of separation, transition, and reincorporation."[5] The rite of separation (ini-tiation) separated the boy from his mother and physically moved him to

2. Ramshaw, *Christian Worship*, 36.

3. As cited in Grimes, *Deeply Into the Bone*, 91.

4. This is not intended to be an exhaustive list.

5. van Gennep, *Rites of Passage*, 11.

another place—out in the "bush"—where he would undergo various trials and learn skills that he would need for the next stage in life. This training was a liminal stage, where the "no-longer-a-boy-but-not-yet-a-man" would be in special non-hierarchical community with others like him.[6] Having learned skills and passed the test, he would be reincorporated into the community as a man with a new social status, new responsibilities, and higher expectations.

Traditional rites of passage for women, however, are different from those for men. Humanities and religious studies professor Bruce Lincoln found that traditional women's rites follow a basic pattern of "enclosure, metamorphosis (or magnification), and emergence."[7] Thus, often at menarche (first menstruation), a girl is separated from others and isolated or enclosed. At this point, she magnifies the skills she already has and may identify with a cosmic or mythical heroine through the stories she is told. Then, she emerges as a woman, one who is able to create and sustain life. As we ponder these two distinct processes, let us consider psychologist Abigail Brenner's conclusion, "While this [enclosure, metamorphosis, emergence] may be true for traditional rites of passage, women today are finding the 'male' structure of the ritual—departure, journey, and return—to be both powerful and true to their own process."[8]

So shall we reject the entirety of the traditional female pattern in order to embrace the entirety of the male pattern for our rite of passage? And how much of another culture's rituals should be transplanted into our non-ritual society? Ritual theorist Ronald Grimes would argue against ritual fantasizing and wholesale borrowing. To think of another culture's rites as idyllic is simply not reality, and to borrow them wholesale is to "cannibalize" them and take "spiritual booty."[9] And while the female process does not sound equal to that of males, there is merit in enclosure and magnification that should not be lost. Why not seek to learn from both? The male process is accomplished in a community of peers, while the female is individual, but our rite of passage, *Woman*, seeks to combine individuality and community; other readers may seek this combination as they journey with friends.

6. Turner, *The Ritual Process*, 139.

7. Lincoln, *Emerging from the Chrysalis*, 101.

8. Brenner, *Women's Rites of Passage*, 21.

9. Grimes, *Deeply into the Bone*, 114.

Unfortunately, we must acknowledge that rites of passage are not always effective—people may remain unchanged.[10] Grimes, however, found that the effective ones have three characteristics. First, they *function* to draw attention to the passage—"spiritually, psychologically, and socially,"[11] and I add intellectually and emotionally. Second, they have the *purpose* of transformation, as from a caterpillar to a butterfly. Finally, they *require* much from the individuals going through the rite and their communities. "Ritual knowledge is rendered unforgettable only if it makes serious demands on individuals and communities, only if it is etched deeply into the marrow of soul and society."[12] Thus, an effective rite of passage *functions* as an attention-giver, has the *purpose* of transformation, and *requires* much from individuals and their communities. *Woman* has these characteristics.

Key Elements of Christian Rites of Passage

I analyzed several Christian rites of passage that are in use today,[13] and this analysis revealed that mature Christian womanhood is realized through relationship, since the rites emphasized relationship with God and with others. This may reflect a common reading of Genesis 1–2 and an implicit understanding of male and female as created in the image of God. Since God is Trinity, and thus in eternal relationship, relationships among humans, whether family, peer, marital, or other, display the image of the Trinitarian God. Though the rites themselves specifically emphasized relationship with God and others, some also implicitly emphasized a relationship with self and hinted at a relationship with creation. *I suggest that the true identity of a woman (or a man) is realized through developing relationship with God, self, others, and creation. The role of a rite of passage into womanhood is to create opportunities for girls to gain knowledge, skills, and a disposition that seeks maturity and development in these relationships.* Though a relationship with self is not clear in Genesis 1–2, relationship with God, others, and creation is. A relationship with self, or knowing and caring for oneself, becomes clear in the biblical injunction to love one's neighbor as oneself.[14]

10. Arthur Magida in *Opening the Doors of Wonder* and Grimes in *Deeply into the Bone* narrate ineffective rituals.

11. Grimes, *Deeply into the Bone*, 5.

12. Ibid., 7.

13. Davis, "Rites of Passage."

14. Lev 19:18, Matt 19:19 and 22:39, Mark 12:31, 33, Luke 10:27, Rom 13:9, Gal 5:14, Jas 2:8.

Since adult Christian women reading the above may consider their own development in these four relationship areas as incomplete, a journey motif for womanhood is also a core principle. The women who lead the rite of passage and seek to help others develop these relationships have not completed the journey of womanhood, for it lasts a lifetime; they are simply further along. A rite of passage invites "younger sisters" to journey together with "older sisters" who offer wisdom and experience and are still continually growing.

Possibly the main function of a rite of passage is to create space to talk about being a Christian woman. Though churches may nurture one's relationship with God and with others, it is often in a generic human sense rather than in a gender-related sense. Christian women relate to God, self, others, and creation in ways that are often similar to other women and different at times from the way men do. A rite of passage creates space where participants are not simply taught to be a Christian, but to be a Christian woman.[15]

Woman is Proven Effective!

In the spring of 2011, in tandem with colleagues, I pioneered *Woman* for a group of seniors at Nyack College. It sought to follow all the above principles, but focused primarily on a woman's relationship to self simply because of the short time frame. The results showed significant transformation,[16] revealing that even this narrow focus also yielded significant growth in the participants' relationship with God, others, and creation. This was evident through comparison of the participants' responses on intake and exit surveys as well as their presentations that defined what being a woman meant to them, made at the final Crossing Over Ceremony.

Allow me to include just a few of the participants' written responses on the surveys. "I've gained much from the mentoring, it really helped me to find and apply confidence that stems from inner strength . . . [and] a strong foundation in God." "One of the things that I gained [through *Woman*] was that power and authority . . . come with knowing scripture

15. Rites of passage for women in traditional societies are mediated by women. Men have a supportive role, because in the same way that men call boys to manhood, women call girls to womanhood.

16. See Davis Abdallah, "Development and Efficacy of a Rite of Passage," for the results of the first year of *Woman*.

and understanding [the Bible]. This was gained through the witness of [the leaders]. The way they were able to use and understand the Word and how it relates to and impacts their lives was so powerful." "I learned that as a woman, I always need to care for myself through proper nutrition. I didn't know how important it was to care for myself before."

Several of the presentations defining womanhood in the Crossing Over Ceremony (the final postliminal celebration) brought out different characteristics of women. As she described the emotion displayed in her detailed and beautiful drawing, one stated, "I think a beautiful thing about women is that we can hold such deep emotion and still go on and still survive." Another stated, "This entire process of being a woman has been amazing, hard, but beautiful all at the same time." Rather than stating negative things about herself, she learned to say, "I'm a woman, and I'm a cool one, too! And it's okay to be confident in yourself because God created us to give what he's given us to other people." "A woman knows her identity, or she strives to understand it, but she does know it's separate from what she can do. A woman lives and relates to God and to others . . . and to herself, from a place of knowing that she's loved and out of loving. A woman will not stop journeying until she understands the core of this—all of this . . . I'm no longer a little girl." All these women named themselves "woman" and gave meaning to the word.

It was a privilege for our community to invest and to walk with these women for that short semester, witnessing and catalyzing their transformation. The attention paid to the passage into womanhood was vital to their journeys, and they have progressed in understanding their personal identity much earlier in life than I did. It is my hope that this transformative process will become accessible to more and more Christian women.

Moving Forward

This book was originally intended to accompany the *Woman* 2014–2015 rite of passage at Nyack College. Now, it is intended to nurture growth in the journey of womanhood for all the women who read it. Lisa Graham McMinn's foreword encourages you to take this journey with friends, and I heartily agree! When the words used are from the *Woman* initiation that welcomes participants to the journey, consider yourselves equally welcomed. When *Woman* assignments are described, join us by also doing them! And be sure to chat about it all as you journey with friends. Here is the path it follows:

Beginnings is the first chapter, and it recommends some overall habits that will help in the entire process of understanding womanhood. The next three sections develop the four relationship areas: with God, self, others, and creation.

Relationship with God addresses general Christian conversion and discipleship, stories of the women in the Bible, what it means to be created in the image of God, and the valuing of characteristics commonly associated with femininity.

Relationship with Self explores how a woman can value menstruation as giving life, accept and love her body, take care of herself physically and emotionally, and spend time alone without fear. It will develop her voice, her confidence, her understanding of sexuality as not limited to genital sexuality, and her commitment to sexual purity.

Relationship with Others investigates healthy interdependence rather than overdependence or over-independence. It will touch on mentoring relationships, relationships with friends (male and female), relationships with older men and women, and romantic relationships.

Relationship with Creation develops the idea that creativity and giving life are part of what it means to be in the image of God. This relationship includes practicing Sabbath, habits of hiking or otherwise being in creation, as well as caring for the earth's resources and assessing one's carbon footprint.

These pages will be peppered with quotes from women who have journeyed before you, whose chorus of voices will join mine to guide and encourage. They will be anonymous, but are either at the beginning of each section or set apart from the regular text as a sidebar. Please receive the quotes knowing that they are from a diverse group of women—ethnically, culturally, and in age![17] Each chapter also begins with quotes whose authors are identified. The quotes are intended to make us ponder ideas

17. Thus far (2014), fifty-seven women have completed the journey of *Woman*. Of those, approximately 21 percent were not college seniors, ranging in age from twenty-three to forty; about 25 percent were brought up in an urban environment, 67 percent were suburban, and 8 percent were rural; approximately 5 percent were Asian, 16 percent were Black (African American), 4 percent were black (non-African American), 16 percent were Latina (from various countries), 7 percent were multiethnic, and 50 percent were white (making 50 percent of participants nonwhite), and two of the participants were international students. The quotes are taken from a random sampling of these women.

together and do not denote complete agreement with any author, celebrity, or teacher cited.

Furthermore, each chapter ends with discussion questions and a prayer. The questions are for you to ponder on your own and to share with others who are journeying with you. The entire prayer for each relationship is at the end of the section, and the prayers at the end of the chapters generally form part of the prayer. Feel free to pray them devotionally.

Though this book is about womanhood, it is not only for women, but also for men who seek to understand and empower their wives, daughters, and friends to be the women God has formed them to be. And for those of us who never had a rite of passage to call ourselves women, may it also be for our personal transformation and inspiration to help those who come after us!

1

Beginnings

Habits for the Journey

Anytime a woman competes with another woman she demeans herself.

~ SHERRY ARGOV, AMERICAN WRITER

The healthy and strong individual is the one who asks for help when [s]he needs it. Whether [s]he's got an abscess on [her] knee or in [her] soul.

~ RONA BARRETT, GOSSIP COLUMNIST

A woman who is not happy with herself can never be happy for someone else.

~ KAMRYN ADAMS, AUTHOR

WELCOME TO THE JOURNEY of womanhood! Perhaps this journey began long ago for you, or perhaps it's just beginning; wherever you are, I heartily welcome you. Womanhood is a journey that is never complete but always growing, never the same but with an ebb and flow, never boring but full of joy, sorrow, and contentment. Womanhood is not a vocation that we attain through hard work, but rather a journey unique to each of us that we receive and live to its fullest. The goal is not to measure where you are on the journey, but rather to be on the path and to walk it with others. The path is not about success or failure—we do not succeed or fail in this journey, because we will always be women.

Paying attention to the journey of womanhood is our primary goal. Though we may in fact be women, if we don't pay attention to womanhood, we will miss the blessings it holds. Throughout the time you spend reading this book, why not make it your goal to pay attention to the journey of womanhood, so that you can receive and live it to the fullest? I recommend developing a few habits that will make the journey enjoyable and smooth; these habits are good life habits that will hopefully stay with you. They are four: I invite you to develop the habits of naming yourself "woman," asking for help, investing in yourself, and embracing your own unique journey.

Name Yourself "Woman"

Language is powerful. The words we use to name things make a difference. The old adage, "Sticks and stones may break my bones, but words will never hurt me," has been proven false through many of our experiences. Words both build up and break down. Words both curse and bless.

When I was a little girl, Mr. Tanner always told me I was beautiful, and I internalized his blessing and never doubted my appearance, though I don't recommend that we value women only for their looks. However, formative people in my life called me stupid, and my intelligence is something I have deeply doubted through the years. In your life journey thus far, it is likely that you have internalized words others have said about you, whether those words have caused you to believe in yourself and love who you are, or to believe you are worthless and unacceptable.

And it's not just words that *others* use for us, but even words that *we* use to describe ourselves. This book is about being a Christian woman, and I encourage you to use the words that describe women in this book to describe yourself. Rather than cursing yourself, bless. As a first act of blessing, I invite you to no longer refer to yourself as a girl, but to refer to yourself as a woman.

It may seem awkward at first, especially if you're not sure what a woman is. If you believe you are no longer a girl, though, you will "grow into" what you call yourself. When someone graduates from college with an accounting degree, she should call herself an accountant, even though she has not yet been employed as one. When she gets an accounting job or consults with businesses, her identity as an accountant will grow, and her journey will likely include continuing education, but she was an accountant even when she lacked experience.

So it is with womanhood. Neither college graduation, marriage, motherhood, nor career give you the name "woman"; only *you* can. God has made you a woman and given you the privilege and authority to agree with your Creator by naming yourself "woman" and forming your identity as a woman. It is within your grasp. If you are reading this book, you've reached a place in your life where you believe that you are a woman, even though you may not fully understand what womanhood means. Reading more and having various experiences will help to define the lifelong journey of womanhood, but the beginning blessing is yours to receive and vocalize. Make it a habit to name yourself "woman" in your thoughts and in your conversations, and you will personally experience the transforming power of language. So, will you try it with me? Sit up, take a deep breath, and say it out loud: "I am a woman!" Feel the waves of strength that name provides.

Ask for Help

The power of naming yourself is yours, as is the ability to receive help from others. You are created to need others, can learn from others' successes and mistakes, and have the opportunity to make it a habit to ask for help. Please understand, I am not suggesting becoming a super-dependent-I can-do-nothing-on-my-own kind of person that asks for help with everything. However, being the I-am-independent-and-need-no-one kind of person repels people, is lonely, and makes life harder for herself.

Don't get me wrong—I can carry a box of heavy items up the flight of stairs to my apartment, use a screwdriver and hammer effectively, change the tires, cook a many-course dinner, compete with anyone on the soccer field, and be successful in my job *all alone*. For a long time, I did all this and more to prove that I could. I only proved it to myself, though, since it didn't really matter to others, and I have later found that life is more enjoyable and easier when others help. Womanhood is not about achieving but rather about being on the journey and walking it with others. Asking for help facilitates this journey and makes it more enjoyable and smooth.

But asking for help does not always come easily. Many struggle with asking, especially for something they really, really want. For them, before even asking, all of the following and more must be answered: Do I really deserve this? Does that person want to give it to me? Can I get along without it? How much will it hurt if he/she says no, and can I handle the pain?

This mental anguish makes the question far weightier than it should be and discourages asking.

In my experience, not only did I not ask for help because I wanted to prove myself, but also because I was ashamed to need help and sometimes I thought that others would not want to help me. While there are bad thought patterns behind these negative ideas that must be worked through, at the end of the day, people don't mind helping. In fact, I *like* to help a friend move, I *like* to throw a party for others, I *like* to discuss decisions, and I *like* to mentor people. So do many other women. This relational drive is part of what it is to be in the image of God, a concept we will further discuss as we move on. Asking for help calls for interdependence, a healthy balance between independence and dependence—a healthy relationship with others.

One way of asking for help is asking a respected woman to be your mentor, a requirement of *Woman*, and a suggestion for all readers. For some, asking is easy, and for others it is quite difficult because the fear of rejection rears its ugly head. When someone is unable to mentor another, it is generally due to lack of time or resources, and not due to lack of respect or affection for the person asking. And the value of the mentoring relationship in *Woman* is consistently applauded. The women asked for help and receive more than they could dream of. They stated the following about their mentoring relationships: "The most difficult thing was finding/asking [a mentor]. But through that, I have been able to become more assertive and brave, and not be afraid to ask people things." "I realized honesty, transparency and vulnerability is most important so maybe I have gained some strength in that area." "I have gained confidence, the ability to process my feelings and a greater sense of self through it. The difficult part was learning to trust that my mentor was not going to judge me." "I told her my darkest, scariest secrets and she loved me and advised me and led me to God." Your mentors and other women around you represent a wealth of knowledge, experience, and love, all of which can help you. Their wisdom is yours for the asking, so ask!

A good friend encouraged me to ask for help with this statement: "If you don't ask, the answer is always 'no.'" Quite a bit of wisdom is packaged here. Generally, when "no" is the answer, we are simply left where we were before we asked. Life is not worse; it is essentially the same. If a "yes" will have a positive effect, and a "no" will have none, why not ask? The worst-case scenario is that life is the same, until you get a "yes" elsewhere. If you don't ask, the answer is always "no," but if you ask, it might be "yes," and the risk is usually worth it. The habit of asking for help will bring great benefit to your life.

Invest in Yourself

The third habit to develop does not require much risk—it is the habit of investing in yourself. Perhaps others have no problem investing in themselves, but when I do, it's often hard to shake off the feeling of guilt. I know many women who have no time for themselves—it seems that women are predisposed to give to others and not to give to ourselves and it's hard to tell whether the source of this predisposition is our nature, or cultural or family expectations.

I watch men spend hours on the golf course, at sporting events, or following some engrossing hobby that is often a financial investment. I seldom see women do the same. Personally, I've been known to often shop at thrift stores, to only buy sale items, order only water at restaurants, vacation "on the cheap," and to otherwise deprive myself, always thinking about how to save both money and time. And I experience a certain amount of guilt when I spend money on myself and it's not for something I need or I judge that I earned.

I remember when I was a poor seminary student and I decided I was allowed to drink coffee at a local café, an activity that was an investment at the time. Even though I could brew it just fine in my apartment, coffee from the café made me happy, and that joy was worth the investment. It was a small investment, one ray of brightness on a day, but I remember the coffee, the aromas in the café, the comfy chairs, and the community I enjoyed as I slowly sipped and savored.

A larger investment for me was buying myself symbolic jewelry. Before I began my PhD program, I bought myself a beautiful amethyst ring to remind me that God provided entrance to the program, and would thus see me through when it was difficult. That ring flashed on my finger, encouraging me as I typed my long dissertation. After each semester of the program, I also bought another piece of jewelry to celebrate the accomplishment, and though it felt lavish, I was investing in and celebrating each step.

The theorists state that in order to be effective, a rite of passage requires the investment of the community. The leaders, the mentors, the alumnae, and friends invest in the participants of *Woman*, and the participants think ahead and save in order to invest financially. Other readers may enjoy being creative in personal and community investment.

> "Self-care also involved investing in oneself. It's totally fine to pamper yourself here and there because you deserve it."

It is important to remember that investing in oneself is different from simply investing in "stuff." The investment is not just financial, for we also invest our time. I invest my time in activities that bring life to my soul: walking and hiking, spending time with friends, and adventures. In the same way as with my money, I decide what is important to me (my values), and invest time and money in them. Balanced self-investment can become a life-giving habit on the journey of womanhood.

Embrace Your Own Unique Journey

Though some might look at my life's journey and consider it great, I am unfortunately more attuned to what I do not have than to what I have. Many times I would have traded my years of single adventures for a family, and my drivenness for a more relaxed life. Certain events I wish had never occurred, and other hoped-for events or opportunities I wish would just happen. Suffice it to say, I have spent time and energy on negative thoughts about my life and my future, often brought on by playing the "comparison game." You know what I'm talking about. We've all played it. We look at someone else's life, whether she is a close friend, an acquaintance, or a hero, and we play the game. We compare ourselves to her, and end up on the losing end. We've invented the game, choose to play it against someone else, and then we lose and feel badly. We do it to ourselves.

I could have entitled this section "do not compare yourself" or "flee perfectionism," but "embrace your own unique journey" is broader and more positive. Embrace it, just because it is yours. It is the unique one God has given you. Rather than thinking about others, refocus to understand and embrace your journey—its past, present, and future. Rather than thinking about what you don't have, think about what you do have—gratitude without comparison is a recipe for joy and happiness. Deeply experience and embrace your own journey.

I noted earlier that I am the only woman of the seventeen faculty members in the college of Bible and Christian ministry at my university. I began teaching with only a masters' degree in a profession that requires a

PhD. My research interests include ritual and womanhood, while theirs do not. I do not fit in. When I started teaching, I looked at others' success, and wanted to teach like them in order to achieve the same success. I tried to present at the same conferences and compete in the same areas, since that was the pattern for my profession. After failing in the areas they succeeded, I finally sat back and decided that I was not hired to be (insert colleague's name), but rather to be the best Amy Davis that I could be. This allows me to respect and appreciate my own journey, focusing on mine rather than on others'. It also helped me appreciate my colleagues' individuality and their professional journeys. Though I could learn from them, I was not to compare myself or try to be someone else. I am an individual in my profession; *I am different and that is good.* Because I know few like me, I must blaze my own path rather than follow others' lead, but that is exciting and adventurous and not frightening or bad, if I choose the positive perspective. I am choosing to embrace my professional journey not *in spite of* its unusual qualities, but *because* it is unusual and because it is my unique gift from God. I will find my way.

Comparing myself and perfectionism in my career is not as destructive as it is in my personal life. I am guilty of playing the "comparison game" with other women with regard to friendships (I never seem to have enough), dating, marriage, physical strength, beauty—you name it, and I've compared. And lost. Every time. She always has/is more (insert anything) than I have/am. The comparison never did me any good.

Few areas were greater ones of comparison than my love life. Though, as I mentioned earlier, I wanted to be married after college, I was single until the age of thirty-nine, and though I generally did not want others' particular husbands, dogs, houses, or children, I wanted their lives. Mine felt empty, isolated, and somehow "less." My journey felt somehow broken, but the lyrics Rascal Flatts popularized rang true and encouraged me even when I felt lack. "God Bless the Broken Road" is about how disappointments and heartbreak in the relationship journey finally led to lifetime love. It gives meaning to all things that don't lead to "happily ever after," because without those transformational disappointments, the road would not lead to the lifetime lover.[1]

I even think this sentiment can be generalized—that long-lost dreams can lead us to fulfillment in never-before-thought-of dreams, that sadness can lead us to joy, and that God blesses that which is broken. Now, when I

---

1. Hummon, Boyd, and Hanna, "God Bless the Broken Road."

look back on my life, it seems to be a straight line—I can see how so many events led to the next and to the next, and finally to where I am, whether in my career or my personal life. In the midst of it, though, I remember losing time comparing and punishing myself for not being perfect. Time that could have been spent embracing my journey and living it well, even though it was different from others'.

Throughout the journey of womanhood, remember your individuality. Do not measure success based on others' journeys; do not become obsessed with wanting what others have. Those habits lead to discontented inadequacy and depression. Name what you have as good, and even when it's pimply and sometimes downright bad, trust that God is leading you. Make it your habit to embrace the journey your Creator is walking with you.

> "When in my fear, I choose to embrace the unknown, an incredible amount of peace overwhelms me, and God's heart is pleased. Through *Woman*, I learned I can only be who I was created to be. I have no other options. Being uniquely me is risky, and yet a risk worth taking; one that apart from Jesus, I could not take."

So, friends, fellow travelers on this journey of womanhood, make it your habit to name yourself "woman," to ask for help, to invest in yourself, and to embrace your journey. Habits take time to develop—no habit develops overnight, so encourage yourself with even little successes because these habits are challenging! When someone treats you like a little girl or calls you a girl, name yourself "woman," if only in your head, and celebrate your step in this journey. When you need help, even in some small manner, rather than barreling through and figuring it out all on your own, ask for help, and celebrate your step on this journey. When your day needs lifting and your soul needs food, invest in that small luxury that gives you joy, and celebrate your step on this journey. When you face disappointment or are surprised by joy, embrace your own unique journey, seeking to deeply know yourself, and celebrate your step on this journey with gratitude in your heart. The more you take these steps, and the more you pay attention to the journey of womanhood, these actions will become habits, and the smoother and more enjoyable your journey will be; you will to receive your journey and live it to the fullest.

And so we begin our journey together.

To chat about over tea, coffee, and/or chocolate:

Which of the habits (naming yourself "woman," asking for help, investing in yourself, embracing your journey) is easiest for you?

Which is most difficult?

What are the barriers standing in the way of your practicing these habits? How can they be removed?

What steps are you taking/will you take to form these habits? Are there any steps you're celebrating?

Prayer

Gracious God, from the depths of my soul, I praise and thank you, for I am a woman of the Trinitarian God. Creator, I praise and thank you, for you have made me to need others. Redeemer Jesus, I praise and thank you, for you have invested your life for me, have counted me worthy of that investment, and given me opportunities to invest in myself. Sustainer Spirit, I praise and thank you for accompanying me on my unique journey that I choose to embrace. Holy Trinity, be forever praised and empower me to do your will.

Amen.

SECTION ONE

Relationship with God

"The four areas of womanhood (relationship with God, self, others, and creation) were all very extensive and eye-opening for me. I believe that all these areas are all connected and not segmented. Therefore, I believe that as I grow in my relationship with myself, others, and creation, my relationship with God will grow as well."

"*Woman* helped me to understand and embrace the fact that I am a woman and to learn how that can be included in my relationship with God."

Introduction

Getting "Behind the Wheel" Spiritually

"Blessed women of God, you have come to develop your relationship with God. In your interviews, you told us the stories of your spiritual journey thus far, and now we journey together, receiving deep personal understanding of ourselves in the image of God, learning and valuing the positive biblical story of women and femininity, and emulating the actions and characteristics of women in Scripture. We welcome you."

THUS ARE THE WORDS of initiation at the first ceremony of *Woman*. As our journey of womanhood is a process, so also is our spiritual journey. It often has a discrete beginning, whether at our baptism, or at a time when we realize our need for God and surrender our lives. Just like a journey across the country, it is accomplished at varying speeds, through differing terrain, punctuated with great views, but with much time spent simply behind the wheel. Being behind the wheel can be boring, but in order to assure a good and safe ride, you need to keep your hands on the wheel, the seat belt on, your eyes alert to your surroundings and the warnings on the dash, and the tank filled with gas.

Though this section is primarily about being in the image of God and the story of women and femininity in Scripture, if we extend the road trip metaphor, you can think of this section as your long stop at Yellowstone National Park that you look forward to and that has a continuing effect on your journey with God. The "behind-the-wheel" basics of our spiritual journey are assumed—keep developing and maintaining those habits. They include habits like asking the Holy Spirit to bring about deep change, learning to study and interpret Scripture, becoming part of the community of Christians, and praying in the Spirit on all occasions with all kinds of prayers and requests.

In our relationship with God, we want change and growth; we want tomorrow to be better than today, and all this is accomplished through the work of the Holy Spirit. So, continue to ask the Holy Spirit to guide you and change you, and pray in the Spirit with all kinds of prayers and requests (Eph 6:18). Any relationship requires communication, and prayer is conversation with God; a verse that always encouraged me tell everything to God is Psalm 62:8: "Trust in him at all times, O people; pour out your heart before him; God is a refuge for us" (NRSV). God *desires* for us to pour out our hearts! God furthermore desires to communicate to us, so be sure to listen as well as to talk.

In addition to praying, both being part of the community of Christians and biblical study develop our relationship with God. Our community must include friends who are younger, older, and our age—people who are walking their own Christian journey. In *Woman*, people have the opportunity to develop relationships with peers who are walking this journey of womanhood with them. All of our lives will be enriched and our journey sweeter and deeper as we intentionally spend time with others and learn from those who are both like and unlike us. Journey together with them, and journey with Scripture, too. Reading and studying the Bible helps us understand how God has interacted with people in the past and gives us insight into how to be a Christ-follower. Your mentor may point you to resources that will help with these "behind-the-wheel" habits. Just like the world around us has winter, spring, summer, and fall, one's relationship with God has varying seasons, and it is important to live in the present with God rather than trying to recreate the past; I find that different spiritual disciplines and relationship habits are for different seasons in my walk with God. I've also found that putting on a tank top in January doesn't make summer come any sooner, so accepting our season is best!

This section is about God's image in us as well as the Bible's depiction of and women and femininity. The fact that humans are in the image of God has a depth that is often unexplored, and the story of women and femininity in Scripture is frequently ignored. As we understand and receive what God states about us, we spend time with God and develop our relationship. Have you ever noticed that people who spend a lot of time together tend to have similar mannerisms, and sometimes even begin to look alike? If we spend time with the triune God, our mannerisms and looks may change as God's image in us is restored from the damage it suffered in the fall.

2

Fashioned and Formed
The Image of God

Becoming one with Christ creates a new identity. Participating in the image of Christ transforms old social identities, grants authority to speak, and bestows worth and value. Women in the image of God means that a woman's face reveals the face of God, that God speaks to women and through women.

~ KAREN TORJESEN, "WOMEN CREATED
IN THE IMAGE OF GOD"

We are made in the image of God; we carry within us the desire for our true life of intimacy and adventure. To say we want less than that is to lie.

~ JOHN ELDREDGE, *THE JOURNEY OF DESIRE*

I REMEMBER OFTEN HEARING Tim Keller at Redeemer Presbyterian Church in New York City state something like, "God loves the city more than the country because God loves people more than trees; in the city there's more people than trees, and in the country, there's more trees than people." We are fascinated by great sunsets or vistas, but they are not created in God's image—people are, so Keller suggested that we walk down Fifth Avenue, gazing upon those created in God's image with wonder, as we would a sunset.

I must admit that I have not walked down a crowded city street and stared, though I have honestly considered it, especially as I meditate on the fact that each person in front of me is created in God's image. When the original hearers of Genesis 1 heard "image of God," they immediately thought about the visible, carved images of the king that were placed all around their city.[1] Just as those images were reminders of the king that was not always there, so also people in the image of God are to remind us of God. And even more, the king's images were thought to contain the essence of what they represented, an essence that enabled the image to do its job.[2] If the person in front of me is in the image of God, containing the essence of God, that changes everything.

Certainly, the image has been distorted, and we are no longer able to consistently act and choose the good and God. However, it has *not* been lost, for the essence remains.[3] When I look at others, I want to be reminded of God, and when others look at me, I desire the same.

Genesis 1:26–27 makes it clear that both male and female are created equally in the image of God:

> Then God said, "Let us make humankind in our image, according to our likeness; and let them have dominion over the fish of the sea, and over the birds of the air, and over the cattle, and over all the wild animals of the earth, and over every creeping thing that creeps upon the earth."
>
> So God created humankind in his image,
>
> in the image of God he created them;
>
> male and female he created them (NRSV).

Perhaps you're accustomed to reading "man" in this passage instead of "humankind." However, though the word used here is the same word used later to describe Adam, it is clear that God is not only speaking of the male since the last sentence describes both female and male. Even if another word is used, the phrase "in the image of God he created them" is identical in practically all English versions, denoting the divine image in *them*.

Both female and male, the two sexes, are in God's image. God created sex, the act, and sex, the distinction between male and female. Since that distinction did not previously exist, it stands to reason that God, who *did*

---

1. Hess, "Equality with and without Innocence," 81.

2. Walton, *Zondervan Illustrated Bible Backgrounds Commentary*, 20.

3. McMinn, *Growing Strong Daughters*, 19.

previously exist, is neither male nor female, but "contains and transcends both," and this is the historic theology of the church.[4]

God is like a father, but is not actually a father, for God is greater than a simple metaphor that denotes close relationship with the divine. God is like a rock, yet is not a rock, for God is greater than a simple metaphor that denotes the dependable and unchangeable nature of God.[5] Metaphor is the only way finite human minds can begin to understand the infinite God, but metaphor is God's "baby talk" so that humanity can understand only as much as the creature can possibly understand its Creator. In analogy, what is unlike is greater than what is like, and the analogy should open one's mind to both mystery and awed doxology of the God who created language.[6] We will explore these ideas in greater detail in the next chapter, with reference to gender (femininity and masculinity).

> "*Woman* reminded me to pay more attention to the things that God says about what we mean to him and what we were created to be."

Humans are Relational

So, then, if we, male and female, are both in God's image, what does that mean? First, it means that we are relational or social, as God is. "Let us" denotes the relational Godhead and being in God's image means that we are to be relational and in community.[7] Psychologist and professor Mary Stewart Van Leeuwen emphasizes that this relational essence is for both male and female when she states, "If God is a social tri-unity whose image is in all persons, then it comes as no surprise to read in Genesis 2 that it is 'not good' for the man to be alone. So God creates the woman. Once they are together, God's clear intention for male and female is equality and interdependence in the context of differing sexuality."[8]

---

4. Aldredge-Clanton, *In Whose Image?*, 57. In this argument, I do not seek to explain *how* creation occurred; I simply agree with the claim of Genesis that God is the ultimate origin.

5. Ramshaw, "De Divinis Nominibus," 121.

6. Ibid., 122.

7. McMinn, *Growing Strong Daughters*, 22; Van Leeuwen, *Gender and Grace*, 39–40.

8. Van Leeuwen, *Gender and Grace*, 40.

Because the image of God denotes sociability, we therefore must be in community in order to develop fully as persons, and though this does not necessitate marriage, that community must include the opposite sex.[9] "God is too big to be captured in any one individual, so God created diversity—male and female, old and young, a multitude of different cultural backgrounds—and it is together that we more completely reflect who God is."[10]

Has a friend's perspective ever changed the way you think? Each of us brings a different perspective that more completely reflects reality and God than our limited personal perspective. We are inherently social beings. When we experience joy with others, when we experience loneliness, when we hold a loved one's hand, we display the essence of the image of God.

Humans are Stewards of Creation

Recently, I received a distressed text from one of my female students. Apparently, she was involved in a heated discussion about Eve, the serpent, and the fall in Genesis 3. She wanted to know if Eve had dominion over the animals since someone had said Eve had not yet been created when the dominion was given. Apparently, they thought Eve susceptible to temptation from the serpent because she did not have dominion over creation. I responded with what any good Bible professor would say: "Read the text." The rest of the Genesis 1 text goes like this:

> God blessed them, and God said to them, "Be fruitful and multiply, and fill the earth and subdue it; and have dominion over the fish of the sea and over the birds of the air and over every living thing that moves upon the earth." God said, "See, I have given you every plant yielding seed that is upon the face of all the earth, and every tree with seed in its fruit; you shall have them for food. And to every beast of the earth, and to every bird of the air, and to everything that creeps on the earth, everything that has the breath of life, I have given every green plant for food." And it was so. God saw everything that he had made, and indeed, it was very good. And there was evening and there was morning, the sixth day (1:28–31, NRSV).

9. Ibid., 41.

10. McMinn, *Growing Strong Daughters*, 22–23.

According to the text of Genesis 1, the female *was* created before they were given dominion, and in fact, this is the second primary meaning of humanity in the image of God; both have accountable dominion over the list above, under God.[11] The functions listed above were typically given only to kings, but here we see that *all people* are given that responsible dominion by God.[12]

Perhaps "dominion" is not the best word, for it sounds too much like "dominate." "Domination" is very far from the biblical picture here. The words suggest harmony, as when the sun rules over the day and the moon over the night (Gen 1:16–18).[13] The sun brightens the day and is the source of warmth and growth. So also, we who are in the image of God brighten the world around us and nurture growth. "Men and women were commanded by God to 'open up' the possibilities latent in the creation."[14] We are all familiar with hidden potential or latent possibilities in ourselves and in others; what joy it brings when that potential is realized! We exercise dominion by opening up that potential and those possibilities.

"Stewardship" is a word often preferred to dominion. A woman whose writing has changed my perspective, Lisa Graham McMinn, writes that we "possess an office of rulership and have been charged to be stewards over creation."[15] *We*, both male and female, possess an office of rulership. McMinn expands on the image of God, stating that we can reason and form conclusions, we are responsible moral agents, and we are creative.[16]

Therefore, women are relational and women are called to steward the earth because women are made in the image of God. Most are all too aware of how this image has been distorted. When the first woman gave in to the serpent, she was not exercising responsible stewardship of creation, not acting in accord with her identity as one in the image of God. Consequently, women tend to put relationships over responsible stewardship, and use the preservation of relationships as an excuse to not exercise their rightful rule.[17] Put in its most basic sense, we become wimps when our

11. Van Leeuwen, *Gender and Grace*, 41.

12. Walton, *Zondervan Illustrated Bible Backgrounds Commentary*, 21.

13. Hess, "Equality with and without Innocence," 81.

14. Van Leeuwen, *Gender and Grace*, 42.

15. McMinn, *Growing Strong Daughters*, 25.

16. Ibid., 20–26.

17. Van Leeuwen, *Gender and Grace*, 46.

relationships are threatened. That reflects a distortion of the most basic elements of the image of God—relationships and stewardship.

And there is no lack of examples of this phenomenon.

In the boardroom, she disagrees with the decision for a good reason, but is silent because her relationships with those around the table are threatened by her disagreement with them.

In order to not disappoint her friend, she spends money the way her friend wants, while she truly feels called to invest otherwise.

Because she does not want to be alone, she invests everything in a boyfriend who is distancing himself—her job, other friends, and family suffer.

Though my heart drops as I remember times I have acted similarly, I am enlivened by the fact that even in the fall, our redemption was laid out for us—the seed of the woman would crush the serpent's head! Christ redeems. I picture us and our distorted image as a beautiful, bright glass chandelier that has been twisted, darkened, and turned upside down. Through the fiery, transforming power of the Holy Spirit, the chandelier is becoming bright once more, untwisted, upright, and restored to its original beauty. We cooperate in this process by acting according to the injunctions and examples in Scripture and history. As we make choices toward healthy relationships and stewardship, God's image in us is being restored!

> "Knowing that the same power that conquered the grave lives in me and shares His image with me, the sex that is often seen as less than, gives me the peace. The peace to know that God thinks of me more highly than I often see myself, in spite of my sex."

Allow me one more thought on how to live as someone in the image of God. If God is ultimately responsible for creation and made us, then God's Word (the Bible) must therefore show us the best way to live. It's like a car owner's manual—if you've ever owned a car, you know the manual that comes in the glove box (yes, even in my most used purchases, there was an owner's manual). My father always told me to read it, though I did not always follow Dad's instructions—I just kept it for when there were problems. Truth is, though, if I want my car to last as long as possible and to run as best as possible, I would read the manual and follow the instructions therein. The manual is created by those who manufactured the car.

In the same way, the instructions and examples in Scripture serve as the "owner's manual for life," given by the One in whose image we are created. Heeding them will in turn give us the best life possible for we are living in harmony with the Creator of us all.

So, are you tempted to walk down a crowded street and stare at those created in God's image? Perhaps not. I hope, however, that you've been encouraged and enlivened by the fact that you are created in God's image and your sociability and skill at stewarding the earth reflect that. May you be continually active with the Holy Spirit in the restoration of God's image in you!

To chat about over tea, coffee, and/or chocolate:

Has anyone ever told you that, as a woman, you are not in the image of God? How did/would you respond to that idea?

How do you see relationality and stewardship playing out in your life?

When have you given up your responsible stewardship for the sake of relationship, thus imbalancing the image of God? If you could do it over again, what action would you take?

How does all this affect your relationship with God?

Prayer

O God, in whose image I am created, I beg you to never stop showing me yourself from glory to glory. I repent of the times I have underestimated your image and actions, please forgive me. Teach me, for I want to know the depth to which I reflect your image. I praise you and thank you for making me a woman.

Amen.

3

Biblical Herstory

Women in Scripture

Charm is deceptive, and beauty is fleeting; but a woman who fears
the Lord is to be praised.

Honor her for all that her hands have done, and let her works bring her
praise at the city gate.

~ PROVERBS 31:19–30

The king of Egypt said to the Hebrew midwives, whose names were Shiphrah
and Puah, "When you are helping the Hebrew women during childbirth on
the delivery stool, if you see that the baby is a boy, kill him; but if it is a girl, let
her live." The midwives, however, feared God and did not do what the king of
Egypt had told them to do; they let the boys live . . . . So God was kind to the
midwives and the people increased and became even more numerous. And
because the midwives feared God, he gave them families of their own.

~ EXODUS 1:15–17, 20–21

So Moses brought their case before the Lord, and the Lord said to him, "What
Zelophehad's daughters are saying is right. You must certainly give them property as an inheritance among their father's relatives and give their father's
inheritance to them.

~ EXODUS 27:5–7

SOMETIMES, IN CHURCH, MY perspective on certain biblical stories is changed through what I hear preached. I remember when, just after Easter, a church I visited was celebrating the women that went to the tomb to take care of Jesus' body—the "myrrh-bearing women." The pastor told their story, about how they met the angel, found that Jesus was alive, and were commissioned by Jesus to go and tell the disciples that Jesus had risen. He then stated that these women were the first apostles—the first sent (*apostello* in Greek) to tell others the most miraculous story ever told. I had never heard them called apostles, and was fascinated and encouraged by the pastor's words.

Another time, the reading was John 4. I like John 4—the woman at the well. Whenever I'd heard it preached on before, it was about Jesus and what it meant to worship in spirit and truth. This time, however, the focus was on the unnamed Samaritan woman. Though from a not-so-good background, she was spoken to by Jesus, believed, and evangelized her whole town. She is a woman to be emulated, according to the preacher, and we should all strive to follow her example of faith and evangelism.

Our theology is deeply influenced by on *what* and *whom* we focus when we interpret Scripture. And sometimes, because we've been taught the story one way, we miss other aspects of the story that are equally valid. I knew that the myrrh-bearing women were sent, but I had never considered that the sending was just like other apostles; I knew the Samaritan woman evangelized, but I had only focused on worshiping in spirit and truth. I want to be stretched in my biblical interpretation with differing and valid perspectives. My relationship with God and my understanding of my role(s) in the kingdom of God are influenced by these women's stories.

Jesus and Women

Primarily, the Bible is a story of God loving people with some people loving back and following and others not. Sometimes it seems that we miss the story, especially its story of women. When we think about a woman's relationship with God, the best place to begin is to understand how Jesus, God in human form, related to women. Looking at the Gospels from this perspective is both surprising and extraordinary.

Women Witness Jesus' Resurrection First

Let us start at the end of the Gospels, when women were chosen to be the first witnesses to the supreme event in history: the resurrection of Jesus Christ. The Gospels are unanimous that it was the women who were the first to be told of the resurrected Christ and to see him. Their original goal was simply to serve and to take care of the body of their friend and leader, and yet their diligence was rewarded when Jesus called them to be the first to "go and tell."

Women, whose witness was considered invalid in courts of the time and who were considered weak by Romans and Jews alike,[1] were the ones Jesus chose as the first to experience and to spread the gospel. Jesus could have gone straight to the road to Emmaus or to the upper room—he was not limited to being at the tomb, but it seems that he wanted to appear to and send the women. Jesus' actions made women's witness significant.

Women are Disciples of Jesus

Sometimes, when we think of Jesus walking on earth, we picture him only with the twelve disciples. Well, the truth is, we usually cannot name all those disciples, but are primarily concerned with Peter, James, and John. Unfortunately, that is a very incomplete picture. Among those who followed Jesus were many women who supported his ministry from their own means as he went from town to village (Luke 8:1–3). At one point, Jesus sent out a group of seventy-two who must have been trained by him to heal the sick and cast out demons, and this group may have included both women and men (Luke 10:1–17). Furthermore, in the oft-quoted Mary/ Martha scene, Jesus commended Mary for taking the position of a student with a rabbi and learning from him (Luke 10:38–42). Jesus also stated that his disciples, those who do the will of God, are his mother and brothers, showing both sexes as disciples (Matt 13:49–50). Thus, quite a few women, too many to name, were disciples of Jesus.

Jesus Speaks to Women and About Women

In a culture where men and women were not to speak to one another unless they were relatives, Jesus speaks to the Samaritan woman at the well,

1. Spencer, "Jesus' Treatment of Women," 139–40; Okorie, "Sexuality," 165.

and she is empowered to evangelize her people (John 4). This theological conversation with a woman directly follows a theological conversation with Nicodemus. The story about the father and his lost son directly follow the story of the woman and the lost coin (Luke 15), and the parable of the Talents follows that of the Ten Virgins (Matt 25), showing that Jesus liked to use illustrations that told the stories of both women and men. Jesus commends the woman with the issue of blood (Matt 9:22, Mark 5:34) and the Canaanite woman (Matt 15:28) for their faith, is anointed by and applauds the actions of a woman at Bethany (Matt 26:6–13, Mark 14:1–9, John 12:1–7), raises a widow's son (Luke 7:11–17), heals a crippled woman (Luke 13:10–17), commends a widow's offering (Luke 21:1–4), and is close friends with Mary and Martha.

In fact, though the Gospels depict Jesus citing several faithless acts of male disciples (think Peter), no specific example exists of faithless women. Certainly, when Jesus addresses all his disciples as having little faith, women were in that number, but they are not singled out. Though women's past acts may not have been faith-filled (think the Samaritan woman), when Jesus interacts with them, the interactions are positive portrayals of those women. Furthermore, though Jesus reprimands Martha for being distracted by household duties, he actually calls her out of the "female role" and into the "male role" of learning at a rabbi's feet as a disciple.[2] And, she has great faith that he can raise her brother Lazarus from the dead the next time he visits her (John 11:20–27). Women are portrayed in an obviously positive manner in the Gospels, and they have deep relationship with Jesus.

> "The fact that my mind has been opened about women and their inclusion in God's intentions has helped me to be aware of my own lens that I had put on scripture, so I think I'm able to read more open-mindedly."

Biblical Women

Having established Jesus' relationship with women, we now move on to specific women mentioned in Scripture who may act as role models for Christian women and their relationship with God and the world. Historically, many Christians received a special name when baptized or confirmed.

2. Keener, *The IVP Bible Background Commentary*, 208.

For many, that name is a character in Scripture or a renowned historical Christian whom they deeply respect and would like to emulate. If I were of that tradition, I would want to be named Mary, for the mother of Jesus, possibly because we can know so much about her.

Mary the Mother

Protestants view Mary with suspicion because they believe that other Christian traditions worship her. For that reason, her role in the life of Jesus has been downplayed in many churches. Recently, however, there has been renewed interest in her, and my study of Mary has been rich and rewarding. *Before you read my interpretation of her story, why not read the original account in Luke 1:26–56 and 2:1–52, John 2:1–12 and 19:17–27?*

Mary is likely an early teenager, promised to Joseph and awaiting her marriage, when the appearance of an angel interrupts her plans for her life. She is told not to be afraid (words angels always say) and that the Lord is with her (words God says to prophets in the Hebrew Bible [Old Testament]). She's told she will be pregnant with God's child, and the only question she asks is how that could happen, given her virginity. Personally, I might have "gone all Moses" on Gabriel if I were her, arguing and asking many questions. But not Mary: she first asks how, and then states her identity as the Lord's servant and agrees to her fate.

What a risk-taker! She agrees to be pregnant out of wedlock in a time when women in her condition would be divorced in a way that brought her great shame, thus almost guaranteeing that she would never again have the opportunity to be married.[3] The pregnancy and the divorce would bring shame not only on her, but also on her entire family. Her words, "I am the Lord's servant . . . . May your word to me be fulfilled" (Luke 1: 38), are not the words of a little kid. They are the words of a courageous woman of God who cares more about her identity as God's servant and about her obedience to God than she cares about anything else. These are the words of a woman of focus and determination.

When Mary makes this choice and states these words, the early Christian writer Irenaeus says that she redeems the negative choice of her ancestor.

3. Ibid., 48.

> For as Eve was seduced by the word of an angel to flee from God,
> having rebelled against his word, so Mary by the word of an an-
> gel received the glad tidings that she would bear God by obeying
> his word. The former was seduced to disobey God [and so fell],
> but the latter was persuaded to obey God, so that the virgin Mary
> might become the advocate of the virgin Eve. As the human race
> was subject to death through [the act of] a virgin, so it was saved
> by a virgin, and thus the disobedience of the virgin was precisely
> balanced by the obedience of another.[4]

Mary's act and words redeem the acts and words of her ancestor.

"And then the angel left her" (Luke 1:38). Whatever proof she has that the baby was from God disappears, and so Mary does what anyone might have done—she runs to her cousin's house. Perhaps it's because the angel had mentioned her cousin, and she thinks she might be safe with her. There, she receives confirmation that she had actually heard God. Her cousin Elizabeth, pregnant with John the Baptist, feels John leap in her womb upon the appearance of Mary, and Elizabeth speaks, filled with the Spirit. She blesses Mary's obedience and the child that would come from it.

And it is after she is blessed by Elizabeth that Mary sings the beautiful poem that we call the Magnificat, whose words echo Hannah's in 1 Samuel 2. She begins, "My soul glorifies the Lord and my spirit rejoices in God my Savior" (Luke 1:46–47). To know Mary, we must realize *when* she declares these words. Does she glorify God when all is fulfilled and everyone under-stands it? Does she glorify God when she's accepted by Joseph? Does she glorify God when Jesus is born? No, she glorifies God before all this. She glorifies God before most people would have even known she was preg-nant. She glorifies God for God's future actions, as though they are already accomplished. What a song of faith! She sees what is not as though it is! Lutheran pastor in Nazi Germany Dietrich Bonhoeffer preached on Mary's words in an Advent sermon:

> This song of Mary's is the oldest Advent Hymn. It is the most pas-
> sionate, most vehement, one might almost say, most revolution-
> ary Advent hymn ever sung. It is not the gentle, sweet, dreamy
> Mary that we so often see portrayed in pictures, but the passionate,
> powerful, proud, enthusiastic Mary, who speaks here. None of the
> sweet, sugary, or childish tones that we find so often in our Christ-
> mas hymns, but a hard, strong, uncompromising song of bringing
> down rulers from their thrones and humbling the lords of this

4. As cited in Webber, *Ancient-Future Time*, 49.

world, of God's power and of the powerlessness of men. These are the tones of the prophetic women of the Old Testament: Deborah, Judith, Miriam, coming alive in the mouth of Mary.

Mary, filled with the Spirit and prepared. Mary, the obedient handmaid, humbly accepting what is to happen to her, what the Spirit asks of her, to do with her as the Spirit will, speaks now by the Spirit of the coming of God into the world, of the Advent of Jesus Christ. She knows better than anyone what it means to wait for Christ. He is nearer to her than to anyone else. She awaits him as his mother. She knows about the mystery of his coming, of the Spirit who came to her, of the Almighty God who works his wonders. She experiences in her own body that God does wonderful things with the children of men, that his ways are not our ways, that he cannot be predicted by men, or circumscribed by their reasons and ideas, but that his way is beyond all understanding or explanations, both free and of his own will.[5]

Mary's words are words of valor and faith. She takes a risk that few would be courageous enough to take, stating, "I am the Lord's servant . . . . May your word to me be fulfilled," and then faithfully proclaims what is not yet as though it is. And this is just the first step.

Mary was the mother of God—God was within Mary, born, and then grew up as a human. The depths of that truth are unfathomable. As a mother, she presents her son to the Lord, is greeted by Simeon and Anna's praise and joy, but is startled by the sword that will pierce her soul. She's not always the best mother, since she does leave her son behind in Jerusalem (Luke 2:41–52), but it is clear that her son Jesus loves her and listens to her as she encourages his first miracle (John 2:1–11). I picture her giggling about the great wedding wine in Cana. Motherhood brought her great joy, but also great suffering. No mother should have to watch her son die. Some of the last words Jesus said, though, were to tell John to take care of his mother (John 19:26–27).

Mary the mother, risk-taker, faith-singer, miracle-encourager—who wouldn't want to be like her? She joins a line of courageous and not-so-courageous mothers in Scripture, the most exemplary of which include Hannah who prayed, received, and sacrificed (1 Sam 1-2), Ruth who followed God and was great-grandmother to King David (Ruth), and Lois and Eunice who instructed Timothy in the faith (1 Tim 1:5). Motherhood, however, is not limited to biological children, for Isaiah cries,

5. Bonhoeffer and Robertson, *Dietrich Bonhoeffer's Christmas Sermons*, 97.

"Sing, barren woman,
> you who never bore a child;
burst into song, shout for joy,
> you who were never in labor;
because more are the children of the desolate woman
> than of her who has a husband,"
>> says the LORD (Isa 54:1).

Many women take faith-filled risks with people who are not their children. They sing and dream of things that are not as though they are. Though biological motherhood is a special role, women can be mothers in the best sense even when they do not have biological offspring. Often, like Mary, the words that they sing are prophetic words, a fact that brings us to the story of another woman, Huldah, a Hebrew Bible prophet.

> "The roles of the women in the Bible are examples for us to follow. We can be as bold and make an impact as those women did."

Huldah the Prophet

Huldah is not the only female prophet in the Bible, for Miriam, Anna, Deborah, and the daughters of Philip are all identified in that role. Huldah's story is found in 2 Kings 22. She is a prophet during Josiah's reign, arguably the best king of Judah because of all his reforms.

At that time, a prophet's work was twofold: forthtelling and foretelling. Forthtelling encompassed telling the truth to the people, and when one reads the prophets, that message was generally that people were sinning and needed to turn back to God. Foretelling involved telling what would happen in the future, which was usually that if the disobedient did not turn to God that they would be destroyed. The biblical books called major or minor prophets are thus divided simply because of their length, not their importance. Just as we do not have a book called "Nathan" for the prophet who confronted King David, we do not have one called "Huldah," but both were very important prophets for their time.

Huldah is, in fact, a prophet during a time when few were following God. King Josiah's two closest predecessors rebelled. The book of the law (presumably Deuteronomy) had not been read for years but was found stashed in a broken-down temple that Josiah was restoring. Huldah, how-ever, is known as a prophet during this time, which is quite remarkable considering that so many were not following God.

She is an important prophet, too. When the king tells the high priest, the secretary, the king's attendant, and others to inquire of the Lord regard-ing how to respond to the book of the law, they go to her. The high priest does not make a sacrifice at the altar and inquire of the Lord himself, nor does he put on the ephod or consult the Urim and Thummin as had been done in the past. No, he probably leads this large and high-powered group directly to Huldah, the prophet. And the story makes no apology for visit-ing a female prophet rather than a male prophet, possibly because it was not unusual. Though Jeremiah and Zephaniah are also prophesying at this time, they are not consulted. It seems that, in the mind of the high priest, Huldah is the best prophet of whom to inquire.

The only background we have about Huldah is that she is married and lives in Jerusalem. She seems to be in communion with God since she does not have to stop and consult God in order to deliver the answer to the men. She knows the words of the Lord and speaks them out directly. She forthtells the negative truth (God is angry because the people have followed other gods) and the positive truth (Josiah has responded to God's word), then foretells the negative future (disaster) and the positive, comforting future (Josiah will rest in peace).

The men she instructs take her words back to the king, and the king responds, calls for repentance and cleanses the land. Huldah is a powerful prophet who gives the words of the Lord to a king, high priest, and other leaders, and the leaders respond to what she says. Because of her prior work, her reputation is known, and she directly speaks both hard and comforting truth. Huldah, who knows God and fearlessly acts as God's spokesperson regardless of the difficulty of the words—hers is an impressive story and a great example for us to follow.

Deborah the Political Leader

Another leader for whose sex the text makes no apology is Deborah, the prophet and judge. Her story is found in Judges 4–5. The time of the Judges was not a good time for the Israelites. It was after Joshua's conquest of the land and before the establishment of the kings. While a judge ruled over a portion of the land, the people followed God and prospered, but after the judge died, the people did "evil in the eyes of the Lord." Some see the state of the people disintegrating during the time of the Judges as a parallel development to the disintegration of their regard for women. Judges starts with Deborah's capable leadership, continues with the judge Jephthah killing his virgin daughter (11), and ends with the Levite's concubine cut up to be sent to the twelve tribes (19) and stolen wives (21).

Deborah is a high point in the narrative, holding court under the Palm of Deborah, deciding Israel's disputes, and sending others into battle against the army that was holding Israel captive. She is the only judge in the book of Judges who is also a prophet, and the land had peace for forty years because of her. The primary story associated with Deborah is sending Barak into a victorious battle against Jabin's army. She tells Barak that God commands him to go and fight, but he won't go unless she goes with him.

Now, this is an odd predicament. Deborah tells Barak that God will give Jabin's army into his hands, but Barak wants Deborah with him in the battle. The reason for his desire is unclear—is it timidity or simply great confidence in Deborah? Regardless, it seems that had he simply gone, the honor of the victory would be his rather than given to another (the valiant Jael). Deborah quickly agrees to his request; they go into battle and they win.

Regarding Deborah's character and valor, commentators Cundall and Morris state, "Barak himself plays a secondary part to this great and gifted woman, and drew courage and inspiration from her presence."[6] Even the early Christian writer Ambrose of Milan states, "It is not sex but valor which makes strong. And . . . no fault is found in this woman, whereas most of the judges were causes of no small sins to the people."[7]

Judges 5 recounts the song of Deborah and Barak, a song that holds her in high honor. She is the one who incited the people to battle their adversaries: "Villagers in Israel would not fight; they held back until I, Deborah, arose, until I arose, a mother in Israel" (5:7). She encourages them to fight and appears an equal military leader to Barak.

Deborah is an impressive political leader. The people come to her for judgment, she defeats Jabin's army, and her legacy to the people is forty years of peace. Courageous in battle, wise in her judgments, and broad in her legacy, she is not a woman who is easily forgotten, and her example is one that we can emulate. Though their leadership is different, the New

6. Cundall and Morris, *Judges [and] Ruth*, 82.

7. As quoted in Franke and Oden, *Joshua*, 115.

Testament teacher, Priscilla (Acts 18:24–26), and Phoebe the deacon (Rom 16:1–2) are also great women leaders who influence others.

Martha the Single Woman

Perhaps it is a surprise to see Martha as an example with women like Deborah, Huldah, and Mary. Martha's example is usually one that women are encouraged *not* to follow, rather than to follow. And perhaps the thought that Martha was single has never stood out in the story. Deborah, Huldah, and Mary were married, but their identity as wives is just background to their identity as individuals. Those biblical examples whose identity as a wife is central are not the best examples in that role (think Sarah, Rebekah, or Leah). Though there are passages that address the relationship of a wife to her husband, and the wife of noble character (Prov 31), biblical women do not seem to receive attention for being outstanding wives, but rather for other personal characteristics.

> "Reading the biblical accounts of women showed me that women can fulfill different roles, even be leaders."

Far be it from me to disparage the vital role a wife plays in the family and in society. One wonders what would have happened should Pilate have listened to his wife's concern for Jesus. And it is probable that many exemplary biblical men had exemplary wives whose stories were (unfortunately) unwritten. I do, however, find it interesting that being a wife does not seem central to the biblical portrayal of many women. Though some may assume they were married, Martha and her sister Mary, Miriam, Moses's sister, and Phoebe (Romans 16) were single, and Lydia (Acts 16) was either single or a widow. In the same way that their identities as wives is not central to the story of Deborah and Huldah, singleness is also not central to the stories of Martha and Miriam. Though marriage was even more common in biblical times than it is today, biblical women are not praised for being wives or stigmatized for being single.[8]

Martha is no exception, and her story is in Luke 10:38–42 and John 11:1–12:8. Martha's problem in the familiar Luke 10 story is that she is focused on the details of hospitality, a woman's job. In first-century Palestine

---

8. Even in Proverbs 31, where the wife of noble character does good to her husband and takes care of her children, the list of all her other work both inside and outside her home receives greater emphasis.

and the Middle East today, hospitality is what one does in order to honor one's guests. Martha is accomplishing what is prescribed by her society, and Jesus breaks social norms when he praises her sister for sitting at his feet as any man (but no woman) would. Martha is distracted by all the details of honoring Jesus and misses *being with* Jesus. "Her activity was not out of place but out of proportion."[9] Later in the narrative, at Simon's house, Martha receives no rebuke for her serving, apparently because her service was more balanced (John 12:2).

Martha was distracted and appears frustrated. Perhaps she wanted to sit at Jesus' feet with Mary, but *someone* needed to get the food ready. If I were her, I might have been annoyed that my sister was where I wanted to be and that I was doing all the work. Perhaps that's why she says (I might have whined), "Lord, do you not care that my sister has left me to do all the work by myself? Tell her then to help me" (Luke 10:40). Jesus says that she's so concerned about other things that she's missing whom she is with and whom she is serving. In the same way, many women are distracted by details and miss what is in front of them. Some single women are working on the details of finding "Mr. Right" and miss both the beauty of being single and the great men and women around them.

So Martha is a negative example in that she does not sit and enjoy, but perhaps she learned from Jesus' words. And showing hospitality for Jesus meant also showing hospitality to his companions who were many, as we have seen. What we miss is that single Martha seems to have her own home and takes care of her sister and brother. We also miss that she had close friends of the opposite sex—including Jesus. The Gospel of John states, "Now Jesus loved Martha and her sister and Lazarus" (John 11:5).

Martha was also more of a go-getter than her single sister Mary. They sent for Jesus when their brother Lazarus was sick and they waited for him as Lazarus died. When Martha heard that Jesus was coming, she went out to meet him while Mary stayed home. As illustrated in her haste to meet him, it seems that Martha had learned the "one thing necessary": to focus on Christ. Though she does not understand everything about Jesus, her faith was clearly very strong for she said, "Lord, if you had been here, my brother would not have died. But even now I know that God will give you whatever you ask of him" (John 11:21–22). When Jesus reveals to her a truth that is revealed to no one else, that he is the resurrection and the life, she confesses her faith that Jesus is the Messiah. This confession is significant—the

---

9. Silva and Tenney, *The Zondervan Encyclopedia of the Bible*, 112.

only other person who confesses the same is the Apostle Peter. Martha is a woman of great faith and intimacy with Jesus.

After she converses with Jesus, she tells Mary that Jesus would like to speak to her. This time, the roles are reversed—Martha spends intimate time with Jesus *before* Mary does, and then she leads Mary to Jesus. Martha was discreet but Mary runs out to him, making the same statement Martha already did, "Lord if you had been here my brother would not have died" (11:32). While Martha's statement had added words of faith, "But even now I know that God will give you whatever you ask of him," Mary's did not. Jesus does not converse with Mary then, but is rather moved by everyone's grief and weeps.

When Jesus asks to have the stone rolled away from Lazarus's tomb, Martha is concerned about the stench, revealing that her faith is still growing. After Lazarus's resurrection, Martha provides for everyone by serving at Simon's house (John 12:2).

Martha is a go-getter who cultivated great faith and independently led her own home, but acts interdependently with her siblings. She is a close friend of Jesus to whom he reveals special secrets. Her faith is strong and growing and she learns from Jesus' words to her about not worrying about material things but focusing on him. She is a great example of a woman, and she was single.

"Through studying several females of the Bible, I learned to find value and lessons from scripture that I had not considered before."

Perhaps you would choose differently from me, if you were to choose a woman for your baptism name. As I've written her story, I find myself especially thinking about Martha. No doubt knowing the story of these biblical women is inspiring, and we've only focused on a few. May Mary, Huldah, Deborah, and Martha continually serve as examples for us as we learn about them, so that we can follow in their footsteps!

To chat about over tea, coffee, and/or chocolate:

What ideas surprised you in this chapter? What are you currently thinking about them?

Which of the biblical women's names would you choose as your baptism name if you were to choose? Why?

How does knowing these biblical women affect your relationship with God?

Read the stories of the following women in Scripture, and chat about them:

Num 27:1–11 (Daughters of Zelophehad); Judg 4–5 (Deborah); Ruth, 1 Sam 1—2:11 (Hannah); 1 Sam 25 (Abigail); 2 Kgs 22 (Huldah); Prov 31; Luke 1:26–66 (Mary and Elizabeth); Mark 5:21–43 (Bleeding Woman); Mark 16:1–8, Luke 24:1–12, and John 20:1–18 (women proclaiming resurrection); Acts 16:11–40 (Lydia); Acts 18 (Priscilla); Rom 16 (great women); 2 John (the lady chosen by God and her children)

Prayer

O God, in whose image I am created, I beg you to never stop showing me yourself from glory to glory. I repent of the times I have underestimated your image and actions, please forgive me. Teach me, for I want to know the depth to which I reflect your image. Remind me of the women through whom you have worked and empower me to emulate them. I praise you and thank you for making me a woman.

Amen

4

Sex and Gender

Femininity and God

God, who is transcendent Spirit, possesses no physical body, yet accommodates to human limitations by using physical, relational, gender-laden images for self-disclosure. Some of those are feminine. Inasmuch as God inspired the biblical authors to be inclusive, who are we not to be?

~ MARGO G. HOUTS, PROFESSOR OF RELIGION AND
THEOLOGY, CALVIN COLLEGE

For this is what the Lord says:

"I will extend peace to her like a river, and the wealth of nations like a flooding stream; you will nurse and be carried on her arm and dandled on her knees. As a mother comforts her child, so will I comfort you; and you will be comforted over Jerusalem."

~ ISAIAH 66:12−13

Courage, sacrifice, determination, commitment, toughness, heart, talent, guts. That's what little girls are made of; the heck with sugar and spice.

~ BETHANY HAMILTON, PROFESSIONAL SURFER, AUTHOR
OF *SOUL SURFER*

For many years, I've desired to visit the Vatican in Rome, to see the great courtyard, to walk among thousands of years of Christian history, and even to visit the Sistine Chapel. Can you picture the Sistine Chapel? I remember learning about it when I was young, and probably the most famous part of Michelangelo's painting there is the hand of God reaching to touch the hand of Adam. God has flowing white hair, a long beard, and a muscular body. And many people picture God like that—a wonderful, powerful grandfather in the sky.

But is that truly what God is like? We are taught that God is Trinity, that God is invisible, and that both of us (male and female) are made in the image of God. How do we reconcile Michelangelo's depiction of God as male, a great man, with the biblical injunction not to make an image of God? And how do I, a woman understand how *I* am in the image of this male God?

The last chapter's mothers and single women, prophets and political leaders are inspirations. And there are even more examples of great Christian women in history. They are strong and courageous leaders, reflecting the image of God in both relationship and dominion.

And they do what God does. In contrast to Michelangelo's depiction, God is neither male nor female (sex) but encompasses both; in the same way God is neither masculine nor feminine (gender) but encompasses both. Several of the words used to describe Mary, Huldah, Deborah, and Martha are traditionally thought of as only masculine: leader, judge, risk-taker, prophet, etc. However, these are clearly positive characteristics as described in the stories, and the Proverbs 31 woman is commended for even more initiative.

Feminine Images of God

The mother image is not far from what God does. Only women give birth, and only women have wombs, yet those images are used of God. Frequently, masculine and feminine images of God are juxtaposed, and for some reason, rather than keeping both in balance, we allow the masculine image to subsume the feminine one. Deuteronomy describes God as one who "shielded [Israel] and cared for him, he guarded him as the apple of his eye, like an eagle that stirs up its nest and hovers over its young, that spreads its wings to catch them and carries them aloft" (32:10b–11), thus using the *female* eagle as a metaphor. In the same chapter, Israel is reprimanded using feminine and masculine metaphor, "You deserted the Rock, who fathered you; you forgot the *God who gave you birth*" (Deut 32:18, emphasis added). Even God's anger can be feminine or masculine: "Like a bear robbed of *her* cubs, I will attack and rip them open; like a lion I will devour them—a wild animal will tear them apart" (Hos 13:8, emphasis added). Moreover, the Psalmist brings both masculine and feminine images together, "As the eyes of servants look to the hand of their master, as *the eyes of a maid to the hand of her mistress*, so our eyes look to the Lord our God, until he has mercy upon us" (Psalm 123:2–3, NRSV, emphasis added).

Scripture also uses wholly feminine metaphors to describe God, especially in Isaiah. "Can a mother forget the baby at her breast and have no compassion on the child she has borne?" (Isa 49:15) "As a mother comforts her child, so will I comfort you; and you will be comforted over Jerusalem" (Isa 66:13). Furthermore, the comfort that the Psalmist finds is to shelter under a God's wings, those of a mother bird's: "I will take refuge in the shadow of your wings until the disaster has passed" (Psalm 57:1b); "He will cover you with his feathers and under his wings you will find refuge . . . " (Psalm 91:4a). Though the pronoun is masculine, the image is feminine.[1] The words *compassion* and *mercy* come from words that mean womb, so compassion and mercy are mother-like. Furthermore, wisdom, thought of as God, is always personified as feminine, specifically in Proverbs 1–11.

Scripture therefore repeatedly uses feminine images for God. If you, a woman, wonder whether God identifies with your struggles or feminine life, know that God gives birth, has pain as a woman in labor, cares for and nurtures others, protects others like an eagle, and is angry like a bear robbed of her cubs. God is not a man or a woman, but encompasses both sexes as their creator. In the second century, Clement of Alexandria wrote the following:

> The Word is everything to the child, both father and mother, teacher and nurse . . . . The nutriment is the milk of the Father, and the Word alone supplies us children with the milk of love, and only those who suck at this breast are truly happy. For this reason, seeking is called sucking; to those infants who seek the Word, the Father's loving breasts supply milk.[2]

Though we may be a little disturbed by the images, they are very biblical.

1. Several of these examples are explained in Aldredge-Clanton, *In Whose Image?*, 24–27.

2. Quoted in Williams, *An End to this Strife*, 68.

Femininity and Masculinity

Although these images in Scripture are clearly both masculine and feminine *biological* categories, it is quite a bit harder to pin down an understanding of masculinity and femininity (gender) as categories in the *nature* of female and male or in their *nurture*. If masculinity and femininity are in one's *nature*, little variation should occur between individuals and across cultures. If they are in one's *nurture*, every person would be different, though there would be some general observable characteristics within cultural groups. Two influential Christian books have stated the masculine and feminine categories are in the *nature* of male and female rather

> "When it comes to Bible interpretation, I want to focus more on passages that highlight the feminine characteristics of God, like being nurturing, caring, emotional, etc., so that I can better grow my understanding of how I am made in God's image."

than in their nurture. When John Eldredge wrote *Wild at Heart: Discovering the Secret of a Man's Soul,* he achieved quite a following and liberated many men. Years later, he assisted his wife, Stasi, in writing *Captivating: Unveiling the Mystery of a Woman's Soul,* which helped many women. They *prescribe* universal masculine and feminine desires as the identity (nature) of the male or female as created in the image of God. According to the Eldredges, the universal masculine desires are three: a battle to fight, a beauty to rescue, and an adventure to live; and the feminine desires are also three: to be romanced, an irreplaceable role in a great adventure, and a beauty to unveil.[3] These desires are how male and female express that they are in the image of God, and those who identified with these desires were healed and liberated through their books. However, we cannot ignore that there are people who do not fit their categories, like a female who identifies more

3. While here I question whether the prescription is a good idea, I also have theological questions about the feminine characteristics. If these are how we reflect God's image, then we should be able to see God having these characteristics. While it is plausible that God enjoys a battle to fight, a beauty to rescue (though the church does not always seem romantically beautiful), an adventure to live, and beauty to unveil, I question whether God longs to be romanced or to have an irreplaceable role in a great adventure. Both those characteristics are dependent and they devalue female singleness or celibacy, a time when one is not necessarily romanced and one has her own adventure. Male celibacy is also devalued since he is not looking for a beauty to rescue. Quite a few reviews question the theology behind the books even though they have helped many people.

closely with the masculine desires, or a male with the feminine ones. Personally, I identify more with their masculine pattern. The Eldredges seem to state that those who do not identify may not be properly reflecting the image of God. Are masculine and feminine really such rigid categories, even across cultures, or can we allow for more individuality?

"The old war cry of the sexists—*vive la différence*—actually implied exactly the opposite: the rigid division of an infinite variety of people into just two categories, male and female."[4] And children's rhymes do the same: "Sugar and spice and everything nice, that's what little girls are made of; frogs and snails and puppy dog tails, that's what little boys are made of." Perhaps you've noticed some distinct differences between yourself and men, but you've also noticed similarities. So, are there rigid categories of femininity and masculinity based on our nature, not nurture?

Lisa McMinn offers a balanced approach. She tends to reject rigid masculine and feminine categories, stating that the reflections of God's image in women are also the way that God's image is reflected by men. God's image in humankind does not change according to gender. However, she would also say that people express God's image differently, and this difference in expression sometimes follows certain gender patterns. She admits that some attributes are ascribed to males, and some to females, but is *descriptive*, not *prescriptive*, in the patterns she observes. That is, she does not make these defining masculine or feminine attributes, but simply describes what is often seen in the North American culture.[5] She also reflects on our understanding of what we see as masculine or feminine, offering a positive solution:

> If we encourage our daughters to be "just like men" (competitive, rational, non-feeling), we are joining the ranks of those who value attributes ascribed to males over attributes ascribed to females. Instead, we need to balance two goals . . . . One is to encourage women and men to regain some of what they deny in themselves because they believe a particular human attribute (e.g., sensitivity) belongs primarily to one sex . . . [T]he second goal is to step away from the trend that sees progress as eliminating differences

4. Tweedie, *In the Name of Love,* as cited in Atkins, *Split Image,* 23.

5. McMinn thus avoids the nature/nurture debate. She acknowledges that some believe these attributes are in the nature of masculinity and femininity, while others believe they are nurtured in our culture. Without choosing a side, she simply deals with these attributes as she sees them, without scrutinizing their origin, and without making them prescriptive for all males or all females (*Growing Strong Daughters,* 33–35, 41).

between the sexes. Instead, we should find ways to embrace those differences.[6]

If we follow McMinn's advice, each woman is empowered to become all she is individually meant to be, not all society thinks femininity should be, because rigid categories are not true to our varied personal reflections of the image of God. McMinn wants women to bring their intrinsic identity to the surface without shame, both when it does and when it does not follow culturally prescribed gender traits.

Devaluing of Feminine Attributes

It is unfortunate, however, that characteristics traditionally thought of as feminine have been devalued by society. This devaluation occurred primarily for biological reasons; it was not a conspiracy. Since women biologically bore and nursed children, their vocation revolved around providing for them through agricultural and other work. Though men helped, they were more free to invent and craft things. Because the inventions directly affected the development of civilization, male work came to be seen as more valuable. This pattern simply became the normative prejudice against things feminine. Society says that masculine rationality is better than feminine sensitivity, masculine competition better than feminine cooperation, and masculine logic better than feminine intuition.[7]

However, if what are often considered feminine attributes are actually part of God's image in humanity, when we devalue them, are we not devaluing God? God reigns with justice *and* mercy. Though they are opposites and at times contradictory, God *is* both. Likewise, God is able to appropriately use rationality and sensitivity, competition and cooperation, logic and intuition.

I remember learning to deny my sensitivity when I was a child. I was very sensitive, and my tendency to cry or to feel things deeply did not get me far in my family or school. I quickly learned to stuff my sensitive feelings under a façade of toughness and tomboyishness.

6. Ibid., 40.

7. Ibid., 36–37. Lisa McMinn brilliantly details this prejudice in *Growing Strong Daughters,* chapter 2: "Masculinity and Femininity." Here, I only focus on specific feminine categories that are clearly like God, and recommend McMinn's work as a more detailed sociological account.

I think sensitivity and emotion are the so-called feminine attributes most devalued by society, but also most clear in God's character. If we read the prophets, especially Jeremiah, God's emotional sensitivity is revealed. Jeremiah is often called the weeping prophet because he expresses not only his own pain over the rebelliousness of Judah, but also the very pain of God. "Let my eyes overflow with tears night and day without ceasing; for the Virgin Daughter, my people, has suffered a grievous wound, a crushing blow" (Jer 14:17). God weeps in Jeremiah.[8] Jesus weeps over Lazarus's death (John 11:34) and longs to take Jerusalem in his arms like a mother hen takes her chicks (Matt 23:37). When Jesus has compassion, as he often does in the Gospels, he is sensitive and empathic like a mother. God is sensitive, and when humans reflect that sensitivity, it is good and valuable.

Whatever our individual differences are, it is best to embrace them and not try to deny them in order to "get ahead," as I did. One goal of a rite of passage is to embrace who we truly are as created in the image of God. McMinn calls for the valuing of characteristics often associated with the feminine, such as intuition, web-based thinking, nonverbal cues, sustained attention to detail, value given to life, and sensitivity to God.[9]

Embracing our individual differences makes us better able to partner in the stewardship of creation, which we should do in all realms of society. Women and men often offer differing perspectives to the same event because they see differently. In the case of the military, while men see the strategy to win, women often see the cost to human life. "Perhaps it would make a difference if an intelligent, capable woman who acknowledged the emotional side of war—that is the concrete reality of the dead and maimed—were the one making the decisions during a military crisis. She could bring a missing balance to the peacekeeping efforts."[10]

Only *both* perspectives lead to a balanced understanding of the battlefield. We are called to steward the creation *together* because only in relationship with one another can we reflect the image of Almighty God.

Though it is dangerous to prescribe femininity and masculinity, it is helpful to discuss them as we see them, and as they reflect the image of God in humanity. Traditionally undervalued "feminine" characteristics

8. Brueggemann, *A Commentary on Jeremiah*, 139.

9. McMinn, *Growing Strong Daughters*, 41–42.

10. Ibid., 45.

of humanity and God can be valued and can thus allow humanity to co-steward creation as those who are in the image of God.

The God of Christianity is sensitive, weeping, and has compassion and mercy like a mother, thus sanctifying a woman's emotions and sensitivity. The Bible portrays this God in both female and male biological categories, illustrating God's anger like a mother bear robbed of her cubs as well as God's birth pains like a woman in labor. These balance, rather than offset, the male categories. This is the God with whom we have relationship.

"I try to take my understanding and acceptance of my femininity, my body and how it was created to a place where I can honor God in it completely, because I accept it for what it is."

Because we can identify as women with God, we can value our reflection of God's image, individual as it is. Jesus valued women, they were his disciples and supported his ministry, were the first to see him resurrected, and Jesus commissioned them to go and tell. Our foremothers, whom we can emulate, include risk-taker, faith-singer, and miracle-encourager mother Mary, courageous and influential prophet of God Huldah, Deborah the courageous and wise judge who left a forty-year legacy of peace, and go-getter, faith-filled single friend of Jesus Martha, as well as many others. Their relationship with God influences ours.

As we journey on, may the image of God reflected by us be restored from the damage it suffered in the fall. May we receive and individually be freed to beautifully reflect the relationality that makes us like God and the stewardship role that does the same. May the Holy Spirit enable us to balance these two and not lose one for the sake of the other. Let us look more like the Triune One in whose image we are created!

To chat about over tea, coffee, and/or chocolate:

Do you see yourself as more masculine than feminine, or more feminine than masculine?

What feminine characteristics that you reflect do you feel have been undervalued? How have you responded to their devaluation? Is that response changing? How?

How does all of this affect your relationship with God?

Prayer

O God, in whose image I am created, I beg you to never stop showing me yourself from glory to glory. I repent of the times I have underestimated your image and actions. Please forgive me. Teach me, for I want to know the depth to which I reflect your image. Remind me of the women through whom you have worked and empower me to emulate them. Help me to understand how my womanhood reflects your image. Name the characteristics in me that you value, and teach me to value them all. I praise you and thank you for making me a woman.

Amen.

SECTION TWO

Relationship with Self

"Self-care is one of the primary things I have learned. Again, we have to work with our bodies. Well-being isn't about wrestling our bodies until they are subdued, but having a relationship with them, in which we listen and respond appropriately. Still learning, but loving the process."

"I have become more aware of who I am as a Woman of God created in the image of God and it has drawn me closer to God as I try to grasp this identity, mostly in times of loneliness."

"I learned how important it is to *pay attention* to my emotions, mental state of mind, and body (what I eat, exercise, etc.). I tend to neglect this and realize how my thoughts have been guided (or influenced) by society subconsciously."

Introduction

Liking Myself

"Blessed women of God, you have come to develop your relationship with yourself. In your survey, you answered questions regarding how you have taken care of yourself physically, mentally, and emotionally, and now we journey together, seeking to understand the rhythms of our body as positive and as an ability to give life, tending to our bodies through nutrition, exercise, and healthy sexuality, becoming aware of our personal strengths and weakness, seeking to build our confidence and use our voice, and dreaming constructively about a future that is tailored to who we really are. We welcome you."

I SAT IN MY office, and she sat across from me. She had thick bangs and long dark hair, which she used, along with a voluminous scarf, to cover her face and body. I'd been mentoring her for a few weeks now, and had discovered an intelligent, beautiful woman who wasn't sure how to use her voice and had little confidence. We had already talked through her bad break-up, and were exploring forward paths.

I asked what she liked about herself, and she turned a surprised face to me. "Ummmm," was followed by a seemingly endless pause. I knew she felt like a different person in different contexts; the college arena did not seem to free her to be "fully herself" and happy. I waited, but words describing what she liked about herself were one or two halting questions: "My hair?" "I am a nice person?" Answers did not come easily.

So I gave her two challenging assignments. First, to write a list of twenty-five things she liked about herself, and then to write a list of twenty-five things she loved to do that made her feel "fully herself" and happy. She left feeling a little overwhelmed.

Perhaps most of us would be overwhelmed when faced with such an assignment. Perhaps we would join *Woman* participants in a stare of fear when we contemplate spending eight hours in solitude with just a Bible and journal. Unfortunately, negative voices can outweigh the positive voices, and loneliness can be crushing. Socrates's "Know thyself" and Jesus' "Love your neighbor as yourself" (Matt 19:19, 22:39; Mark 12:31, Luke 10:27, NIV) call for self-understanding, self-love, and self-respect.

This section focuses on understanding our sexuality, physicality, confidence, and voice in order to develop our relationship to ourselves. We begin with a portion on loneliness, a state with which so many struggle. We will explore how we are physically created to partner with God in giving life, taking care of our physical bodies, and developing our ability to speak and pursue life in confidence. Humans, created by God, are worthy of being loved by God! If God, the almighty Creator of the universe, knows and loves me, then who am I to not love myself and know myself?

5

Alone *and* Lonely

Can the Two Be Separated?

It is strange to be known so universally and yet to be so lonely.

~ ALBERT EINSTEIN

Women need real moments of solitude and self-reflection to balance out how much of ourselves we give away.

~ BARBARA DE ANGELIS, RELATIONSHIP EXPERT

We, who are so schooled in the art of listening to the voices of others, can often hear our own voice only when we are alone . . . . For many women, the first choice, then, is to give ourselves the necessary time and space in which to renew our acquaintance with our lost voice, to learn to recognize it, and to rejoice as we hear it express our truth.

~ FLORENCE FALK, *ON MY OWN: THE ART OF BEING A WOMAN ALONE*

The best remedy for those who are afraid, lonely, or unhappy is to go outside, somewhere where they can be quiet, alone with the heavens, nature, and God. Because only then does one feel that all is as it should be.

~ ANNE FRANK

I USED TO TAKE after-work, winter walks with God. I would go to the corner coffee shop after work, get some of their special hot chocolate, and walk down to the pier and around town. I did it because coming home to an empty one-bedroom apartment was at times difficult for me, and the walks helped. They did not, however, assuage my deep desire for companionship. Once, I wrote a song that demonstrates a desire for a companion, but still questions whether I would really be fulfilled with one:

Taking a walk to Starbucks alone
Maybe I'll see someone I know,
And maybe I won't

On a Sunday afternoon, so many fun things to do,
But there's so much time,
When you're alone

Went to church this morning with friends
And I had a party this afternoon
People coming over tonight
Somehow, it doesn't feel right
But what else is there to do?

I want love, I want you
I want the touch of a tender hand,
Someone to talk to and understand
But where are you?

I think about not being alone
About a cozy apartment made for two
But would that really make me content
Or would I always be bent
On needing something new?

I think I want some kids and a home
Coffee shop and a playground to walk to
A dining room full of friends
Togetherness without end
Alone, is there much more to walk through?

> I still want love, I want you
> I want the touch of a tender hand,
> Someone to talk to and understand
> But where are you?

Even as I remember these lyrics, I recall the feeling when my loneliness would overwhelm me.

In a world filled with smartphones, social networks, coffee shops, and Skype, people are still incredibly lonely. Sitting in the coffee shop with a friend, she texts her boyfriend, uploads a picture of her coffee and snack to Facebook, and receives a Skype call from across the world, all while sort of paying attention to the person sitting across from her. "Usually we are at one place, across from a person, but our hearts are elsewhere."[1] When we are only present with others in body and not in mind, we are lonely.

When single, we like to encourage ourselves in our times of loneliness that someday our "loneliness problem" will be "fixed" by that special someone. While that may make us feel better in times of discouragement, it sets us up for unrealistic expectations and disappointment in the future, since no person can truly fill our void. In the most ultimate sense, we all sleep alone, and "No relationship, however deep, can ever fully take our loneliness from us."[2]

And so young Christian women take the cue from older ones to be as busy and restless as possible, to avoid *feeling* the loneliness, and to avoid being alone. *Woman* participants are unanimously lonely and unanimously afraid of their assignment of spending eight hours in solitude. Yet being lonely and being in solitude are different from one another.

Ronald Rolheiser, in *The Restless Heart: Finding Our Spiritual Home in Times of Loneliness*, explores several different kinds of loneliness. We can usually fit ourselves primarily into one type. First is the loneliness of alienation, the kind where we find our interpersonal relationships inadequate and that frustrates us. Most of us have either watched or experienced the alienation caused through bullying. People are ostracized or different for varying reasons, and that makes them lonely and alienated.[3]

Another type of loneliness is that of restlessness. This is the kind where we are "never satisfied, but always restless; never quiet, always wanting

1. Rolheiser, *The Restless Heart*, 23.
2. Ibid., 18.
3. Ibid., 42–44.

more of everything."[4] Regardless of how our lives look, how many relationships we have, how much social activity we enjoy, it is never enough; we are never content. We are restless, dissatisfied, always pushing to do more—to break through and to break out.[5] Perhaps you've guessed that this was my type of loneliness because of my song above. I clearly had social activity, but found myself restless and wondered if a life companion would actually make me content.

In order to illustrate the next type of loneliness, that of fantasy, Rolheiser tells the story of a priest in an airport who had himself urgently paged so that everyone would know who he was. The priest wanted everyone to think he was important and available in case anyone in the crowd had need of him.[6] The priest had a fantasy that he could save those in the airport and that he was integral to many lives. The way he understood himself and the way he really was were two different pictures. Because he projected a "false self" he was lonely and disconnected to reality. Others can perceive our projection of the fantasized self, and rather than attracting them, it often pushes them away.

The final two types of loneliness are the loneliness of rootlessness (lack of belonging anywhere) and psychological depression. Though we may not all suffer from the final two types, we all suffer from the first three to one degree or another. As I stated above, I primarily suffer from the loneliness of restlessness, and realizing this fact has freed me. When I learned that most people who feel things very deeply suffer from the loneliness of restlessness, I began to accept my loneliness as a "normal" part of my identity.

> "In times of loneliness and pain it's okay to be in that place and in that place crave real intimacy, as bad as it hurts to avoid false intimacy."

I had already realized that being with people or in a romantic relationship did not solve my "loneliness problem." Thus, when I was instructed, when feeling lonely, to go into solitude, pray, and wait until I hear God lovingly call my name, I was ready to try it. And though often difficult to do, it has helped me develop a sense of self.

I want real intimacy, and I'm not talking about the physical kind. I want to know and be known completely and to be free to be my best

4. Ibid., 51.
5. Ibid., 53.
6. Ibid., 60–62.

and worst self. I want to feel deeply connected on all planes. I suppose most of us are like that, and most of us realize that this longing is only fulfilled in short bursts of time, giving us only sporadic tastes of deeply intimate euphoria. Most of life is lived in between those moments, and we spend time desperately seeking them, often through the false intimacies of masturbation or casual sexual acts, just being at social events or social places (coffee shops, bars, etc.), or otherwise avoiding *feeling* the fact that we deeply want real intimacy and do not have it. Everyone else looks so happy and fulfilled, so we falsely assume there is probably something wrong with us and we fear what that might be. Solitude makes us look at ourselves, and only when we look with the compassionate God calling our name, who knows even the hair on our heads, can we love ourselves and embrace our stories.

I'm not sure that we ever fully know ourselves in this mortal life—it seems to me that there are always surprises or more to know with every new experience. It is important, however, that a woman begin the process of knowing and appreciating herself, and that task is accomplished in part by admitting loneliness, not choosing the false solution of restlessness, and learning solitude. Next time you feel lonely, don't try to solve the problem by being with people, but allow yourself to be alone, and wait for Jesus to call your name. It may take longer than you desire, but the rewards will last far longer than the short-lived social event. It is okay to want deep intimacy, not have it, not choose false intimacy, and sit in the longing. God meets us there.

Indeed, when we do not admit our loneliness, we miss its potential value. My times of deepest loneliness were the times when I wrote poetry and songs with increased creativity, and those times of pain helped me to be more empathetic to others' pain.[7] Loneliness "can teach us how to cry, and by that very fact, sensitize us to all that is deepest, softest, and most worthwhile inside ourselves."[8] Paying attention to our loneliness and being in silence and solitude allow us also to share in the loneliness of Jesus,[9] whose friends slept at his time of greatest need (Matt 26:36-46, Mark 14:32-42, Luke 22:39-46).

> "I learned to be still and know that he is God."

7. Although I personalize the potential value of loneliness, they are all listed in Rolheiser's chapter entitled "The Potential Value of Loneliness," in ibid., 130–49.

8. Ibid., 135.

9. Ibid., 148.

Various historical rites of passage have emphasized times of silence and solitude. Lisa McMinn tells the story of a more modern vision quest for Sarah at her menarche (her first period);[10] she spent time alone in a deserted cottage and was transformed. This is a delightful combination of the male rite pattern of separation, and the female rite pattern of being enclosed. Though silence and solitude are sometimes difficult to find, and are spiritual disciplines many prefer to avoid, writers on the spiritual life state that spiritual growth is hindered without them.[11] Silence and solitude not only increase one's relationship with self, but also with God.

It has often been said that each human has a hole inside that only God can fill. If this is true and if God is infinite, that hole inside us is an infinitely deep hole that is never infinitely full, at least on this earth. We will always feel that we are lacking something. Loneliness is thus neither scary nor sinful, but rather a part of the human condition that some feel more than others. This truth may encourage women to face loneliness and experience solitude in order to develop their relationship with themselves.

> "I am more willing to go on adventures and spend that time with God."

To chat about over tea, coffee, and/or chocolate:

What is it like when you are lonely? How would you describe it?

Which type(s) of loneliness do you experience?

What do you try to do to "solve" your "loneliness problem"? When you try to stay alone and wait for Jesus to call your name, what happens?

Spend eight hours alone with only your Bible and a journal, then chat about the difficulties and joys of the experience.

How does all this affect your relationship with yourself?

---

10. McMinn, *Sexuality and Holy Longing,* 16.

11. *Catholic Encyclopedia,* as cited in Jones, *The Sacred Way,* 39.

Prayer

Holy Spirit, you who are called the Comforter, I ask you to comfort me in my loneliness. Transform me into a woman that runs to you rather than to short-lived social pleasure. Please teach me what all of this means and guide me not into temptation. Jesus, you called the people to love their neighbor as themselves, and while I seek to love others, help me to love myself. I pray all this in the name of the Father, Son, and Holy Spirit.

Amen.

6

Body Parts and Life-Giving Red

Embracing Our Sexuality

I don't mind being burdened with being glamorous and sexual. Beauty and femininity are ageless and can't be contrived, and glamour, although the manufacturers won't like this, cannot be manufactured. Not real glamour; it's based on femininity.

~ MARILYN MONROE

"For your information, Lester, there are at least five wonderful parts of the female body that can be viewed by the owner only with a hand mirror."
And as they stared after me, I went regally back down the hallway and up the stairs to Dad's room.

~ PHYLLIS REYNOLDS NAYLOR, *THE GROOMING OF ALICE*

A woman brings so much more to the world than birth, for she can birth discovery, intelligence, invention, art, just as well as any man.

~ SHANNON CELEBI, *SMALL TOWN DEMONS*

HER HEART STARTED TO race and her body to perspire when they laid a diagram of the female reproductive anatomy on the table before her. Fear and anxiety began to overwhelm her as she remembered her pain.

She'd had surgery at eleven. She couldn't remember the name of the problem, but she had been in horrible pain for a full week. Something was stopping her blood from coming, and the surgery released it.

The doctor had coldly put her hands on her private parts and reached inside with a metal scope that hurt. Though she was put out for the surgery, she remembers the pain of recovery. She went back for a checkup and they said everything was okay and she started menstruating normally.

But everything wasn't okay. She didn't understand, she needed to talk, but didn't know how; any thoughts of sexuality brought up anxiety and fear, so she tried to ignore them as best she could.

And then, at the *Woman* meeting, I placed a diagram of the female anatomy in front of her. Her heart raced and her palms were clammy throughout the exercise, but she knew she needed help. She asked to meet with me and talk about sexuality in order to transform her understanding. And though it took time and effort, the anxiety and fear melted away as she began to embrace her sexuality.

Most of us have different views and experiences when it comes to sexuality. Christian youth are taught to delay sex until marriage, and yet are often not given any space to discuss sexuality. Unfortunately, it seems that we buy into the idea that sexuality is limited to sexual intercourse, a topic discussed in more detail in the "Relationship with Others" section. Sexuality, however, is not just sexual intercourse, for we are all sexual— from birth! And sex literally means "to be cut off or incomplete" and is thus connected to our loneliness. We are cut off (sexual), and our sexuality is our need to be connected.

> Sexuality is the drive for love, communion, community, friend-ship, family, affection, wholeness, consummation, creativity . . . joy, delight, humor, and self-transcendence. It is not good to be alone . . . . Sexuality is a beautiful, good, extremely powerful, sa-cred energy, given us by God and experienced in every cell of our being as an irrepressible urge to overcome our incompleteness, to move toward unity and consummation with that which is beyond us.[1]

Genital sexuality is just part of the larger drive for consummation. Roman Catholic priest Ronald Rolheiser intimates that we long for completion, for the "beautiful symphony" to reach its complete climax, but even sexual intercourse does not fully provide it. His "bigger picture" perspective of

---

1. Rolheiser, *The Holy Longing*, 194–95.

sexuality allows all women to understand themselves as sexual even if they are not having sexual intercourse or even in a romantic relationship.

This is not to exclude a woman's understanding and respect of her genitalia, however. While boys believe their penises are treasures and have looked at them and touched them, most Christian girls identify everything "down there" as their vagina, have little idea of what it actually looks like, and think it's dirty. Though they might masturbate, they generally keep it secret. A Christian woman can be empowered to name her external and internal reproductive anatomy correctly because she has been uniquely created by God and her entire being is not dirty but good. It is even helpful to find a chart of the female reproductive anatomy and learn the words and functions for each part. Also, though it may feel strange, it is good to take a mirror and see what you actually look like.

"I gained a greater appreciation of my body and how it is capable of doing so many things, especially sexuality as a woman. I got to say that I haven't looked at the different parts of the female organ before this and it made me more comfortable about the different functions."

Besides knowing straightforward facts about our bodies, masturbation is an act that we can talk about. Not everyone masturbates, but some do. If they do, they often do it when they are sad or lonely and there is a sense of shame connected to it. Although masturbation achieves momentary relief, most realize that it does not solve their sadness or loneliness. After the self-induced orgasm, nothing has changed, and sometimes they feel even worse. We encourage women to embrace their sadness or loneliness as a reminder that they need God and others.[2] When faced with a desire to masturbate, we might try to figure out what is underneath the desire—what lack we are feeling. Understanding the lack, then, we may seek to fill it in a longer-term manner, rather than with short-lived pleasure. When what we lack cannot be filled, we can also learn to embrace it, wait for Jesus to call our name, and choose to be okay.

2. McMinn elaborates on masturbation in *Sexuality and Holy Longing*, 60–63.

Menstruation

Christian women need to know that sexuality is not just sexual intercourse and must also learn to value their bodies. Personal devaluation is most clear in a woman's perspective on her menstrual cycle. I remember when I first started my period—I was actually quite angry that it had begun. I was a teenager, so I knew that it was coming soon, but its advent was not happy for me, and I wanted to fight it.

A woman experiences her rites of passage in distinct physical ways. Menarche (first menstruation), pregnancy, childbirth, and menopause physically move her from one phase to another. Although pregnancy and childbirth are celebrated, menarche and menopause are often associated with shame and either dirtiness or deterioration. It would be of great benefit to Christian women to pay positive attention to these two passages. Since the focus of this text is women who are between these two passages, appreciating one's menstruation is the focus here. Sociologist Lisa McMinn, in *Sexuality and Holy Longing*, laments the devaluing of menstruation in Western society, stating,

> The collective shame and hate of menstruation that women share has emerged partly out of a long-running history of considering femaleness inferior to maleness. Many cultures considered female sexuality not only as being dangerous but as causing women to be frail, irrational, and illogical. By the time humanity reached the Victorian era, Western women had long accepted femaleness as a curse to be borne but not celebrated.[3]

A close look at Genesis 3 shows that God did not curse the man or the woman, but rather cursed the serpent and the ground. That women would have pain in childbirth was a result of the fall, not a curse from God. Still, Christian and non-Christian women alike refer to menstruation as "the curse," are ashamed of it, and pharmaceutical companies regularly offer effective ways to avoid it. We must learn to bless our bodies rather than curse them, and to celebrate that we are uniquely created to give life.

Giving Life

A woman can give life in a way distinct to her sex. She is able to carry a child for nine months and bear the excruciating pain of labor for the

3. McMinn, *Sexuality and Holy Longing*, 16.

joy that comes after it. A Christian woman can identify with the Virgin Mary—the one whom God chose to partner with in bearing Jesus, who was God. And even if a woman does not have the ability or opportunity to bear a child, perhaps she can identify with Jan Meyers in her conversation over coffee with her friend, Brent Curtis:

> Suddenly, he became very earnest. When Brent got earnest, he would slightly cock his head, and it would shake with a small tremor as he waited for a response. He asked me, "How *are* you?" He really wanted to know. My threshold wasn't especially high that day, and I teared up. I tried to explain the difficulty of continuing day to day as a single woman, especially as I give of myself in the counseling office, fighting for other people's marriages.
>
> Brent listened and leaned forward, and with simple focus, he said, "Jan, I'm so sorry that you are having to give life this way." He knew my longings for marriage and children. "But one thing is sure," he said. "You will have a very special place in heaven."[4]

God gave woman the capacity to bear the weight—the heaviness and the pain—and the waiting—the time—in order for God to give life to the Redeemer, partnering with the life-giving woman. And this giving life, as attested above, is not simply for biologically giving life, but also for giving life to nieces, nephews, others in the community, a business, new recipes, plants, children—the list is endless! Menstruation can be a time for a woman to come away, reflect, and remind herself that God wants to partner with her in giving life to redemption.[5]

Our Cycles

Menstruation may also be a time to remember that some things are completed. We have the gift of realizing a beginning and an end every month, and the privilege to reflect. That reflection may lead to contentment, or to a change in behavior so that ensuing months look different. Much of life flows quickly forward, and we have little "built-in" time to reflect back and

4. Meyers, *The Allure of Hope*, 102–3.

5. I do not intend to lightly pass over the deeply painful subject of the limitations women experience in the area of biologically giving life. I'm not sure how to acknowledge that heartbreak while also stating that women are created to give life in a way unique to their gender, even when they are physically limited. Perhaps it helps to think that menopause does not stop a woman from giving life. While that does not take away the pain, it may offer an encouraging perspective.

then look to the future. Women's bodies, however, tell us to do so, and we are benefited when we listen to them! I've often thought of wearing a festive red dress when I have my period to celebrate this time of completion and reflection.

Besides taking time away to reflect, women can also understand how their bodies work at other times in their menstrual cycle. This information can be empowering and freeing. I recently married, and because I like to do things naturally, I chose FAM, the Fertility Awareness Method, for birth control and pregnancy achievement. As I read *Taking Charge of Your Fertility*, I found myself absolutely amazed at how the female body works and how completely ignorant I was. I couldn't believe how much I *could know* and how much I had *never known* about my own body and how it had been functioning for so many years. I felt frustrated and deceived.

I had been taught that a woman's menstrual cycle is twenty-eight days long, we ovulate on day fourteen, and any irregularity was bad and could be solved by "the pill." However, through my reading, I learned that a "normal" menstrual cycle could be anywhere from twenty-one to thirty-six days long and the luteal phase (phase after ovulation) is almost always twelve to fourteen days. That means that if a woman has a twenty-one-day cycle the woman is probably ovulating on day seven, and for a thirty-six-day cycle, she ovulates on day twenty-two. Rather than guessing about whether or when I ovulated, however, I could simply track my waking temperature or cervical fluid and *know*. In doing so, I learned that I had a short luteal phase (seven days instead of fourteen), and that this condition may be due to a high level of the hormone prolactin. So, I visited my gynecologist and told her about my observation, and though she thought high prolactin was unlikely, she reluctantly gave me a blood test. Sure enough, I had accurately self-diagnosed; my prolactin level was too high and I was put on medication to lower it so that my hormones were balanced. Granted, we are not always correct in our self-diagnoses (please note that I was using a published book, not an online blog to figure this out), but understanding how our bodies work empowers us to take care of them.

I find it extremely important to agree with rather than fight with my physical body. In the past, I have tended to do the latter. Rather than agreeing with my body and sleeping when tired, I have fought with it and made myself stay up and accomplish tasks. Rather than agreeing with my body and stopping eating when I'm full, I have fought with it and filled myself to sickness; at other times, rather than agreeing with my body and giving it the nutrients it needs, I have fought with it and deprived it. Rather than agreeing with my body and stretching when I feel tight, I have fought with it, stayed seated, and downed another cup of coffee. My body is my constant companion—fighting with it makes my experience of life worse, but agreeing with it helps me.

While it is not okay to use one's menstruation as an excuse to be mean to others (the fruit of the Spirit does include self-control), if we are tired when we menstruate, it is okay to dial back our activities and take time to meditate and take care of our bodies. When we push ourselves, we pay for it later. Some would say that if we agree with our bodies now and rest during this time that it will have a cumulative positive effect on our cycles; on the other hand, if we continue to push through it all, there is a cumulative negative effect. *Woman* participants chart their cycles, recording moods, eating habits, sleep patterns, energy levels, etc., at various times of the cycle.[6] The following is the chart that we use:

6. The tables are adapted for them from the fertility charts in Weschler, *Taking Charge of Your Fertility.*

Table 1: Blank Menstrual Cycle Chart

CYCLE DAY	1	2	3	4	5	6	7	8	9	10	11	12	13	14	15	16	17	18	19	20	21	22	23	24	25	26	27	28	29	30	31	32	33	34
DATE																																		
Exercise (describe)																																		
Travel (Y/N)																																		
Stress (H/M/L)																																		
Creativity/ Energy Level (H/M/L)																																		
Sleep (number of hours)																																		
Illness (Y/N; Describe																																		
Medicine																																		
Food: Fasting (F) Overeat (O)																																		
Irritability (H/M/L)																																		
Anxiety (H/M/L)																																		
Content- ment (H/M/L)																																		
Ovulation Pain (Y/N)																																		
Menstruation																																		
Spotting																																		
Breast Self-Exam						X																												

Because filling out the chart can be complex, I have included an example chart for someone who had a twenty-four-day cycle on the next page. This person is accustomed to having a longer cycle, but if you study the chart, you can see why her cycle was shorter. Take several minutes to peruse both the chart and the following observations about the chart:

- She started menstruating on 1/9 and bled for the first five days. She also spotted (had a small amount of blood) when she ovulated; this happens with some women and not with others.

- She exercises about three times a week.

- She did her breast self-exam on day seven; since one's breasts are least affected by hormonal fluctuation this day, it's the best day to do it.

- Her creativity and energy levels were highest in the middle of her cycle, and she needed less sleep at the same time.

- She needed more sleep at the beginning and end of her cycle.

- She was more anxious and irritable at the end of her cycle than at any other time.

- She tended to overeat both when she ovulated and close to the end of her cycle (when she was about to menstruate again).

- Her luteal phase (time between ovulation and menstruation) is still about fourteen days, since she had ovulation pain on days ten to eleven, likely ovulating on day eleven.

- Since her cycle is usually longer, we can figure out why it was shorter. Here, her travel and stress on days seven to nine seems to have made her ovulate earlier than usual, thus shortening her cycle. It's helpful to record travel, stress, illness, etc., because they can cause one to ovulate earlier or later, thus shortening or lengthening one's normal pattern.

Table 2: Example Menstrual Cycle Chart

CYCLE DAY	1	2	3	4	5	6	7	8	9	10	11	12	13	14	15	16	17	18	19	20	21	22	23	24
DATE	1/9	1/10	1/11	1/12	1/13	1/14	1/15	1/16	1/17	1/18	1/19	1/20	1/21	1/22	1/23	1/24	1/25	1/26	1/27	1/28	1/29	1/30	1/31	2/1
Exercise (describe)	None	Ran 3	None	Ran 3	None	None	Ran 3	None	Ran 3	None	Ran 3	None	None	Ran 3	None	Ran 3	None	Ran 3	None	None	Ran 3	None	Ran 3	None
Travel (Y/N)								Y	Y	Y	Y	Y												
Stress (H/M/L)							Y	Y	Y	Y	Y	Y												
Creativity/ Energy Level (H/M/L)	M	M	M	M	M	H	H	H	H	H	H	H	H	M	M	M	M	L	L	L	L	L	L	L
Sleep (number of hours)	9	9	9	8	7	7	6	6	7	7	7	7	7	8	7	8	7	8	7	8	7	8	8	9
Illness (Y/N; Describe)	N	N	N	N	N	N	N	N	N	N	N	N	N	N	N	N	N	N	N	N	N	N	N	N
Medicine																								
Food: Fasting (F) Overeat (O)							O	O													O	O	O	O
Irritability (H/M/L)	L	L	L	L	L	L	L	L	L	L	L	L	L	M	M	M	M	M	M	M	M	H	H	H
Anxiety (H/M/L)	L	L	L	L	L	L	L	L	L	L	L	L	L	M	M	M	M	M	M	H	H	H	H	H
Contentment (H/M/L)	L	L	L	M	M	M	H	H	H	H	H	H	H	H	H	H	H	M	M	M	M	L	L	L
Ovulation Pain (Y/N)									Y	Y														
Menstruation	X	X	X	X	X																			
Spotting							X			X														
Breast Self-Exam																								

Some prefer phone or tablet apps; personally, I prefer a paper-and-pencil method because I can see everything all at once. Regardless of how it's done, distinct patterns emerge for the women after recording for several months. This method of self-awareness helps them interpret reasons for particular personal patterns and adjust their behavior in order to care for themselves well. When we do not care for ourselves, we cannot properly interact with others.

> "I think I have an appreciation for my cycle now that I can anticipate its happenings. I try my best to cooperate with it, and make necessary adjustments to keep my body happy."

In addition, while we may be encouraged to draw back when menstruating, we may also be encouraged to go "full on" during other times when we find ourselves particularly creative or strong. Again, why not agree with our bodies and take advantage of the creativity they give us? If we were to display what is often the pattern of women, it would look like the following chart. If your cycle is longer or shorter, you may adjust your thinking accordingly.[7]

---

7. The information in the table is adapted from Northup, *Women's Bodies*, 105–10, 123–25, 136–37.

Table 3: Menstrual Cycle Trends

CYCLE DAY	1-5 (Approximate)					6-14 (Approximate)									15-28 (Approximate)													
	1	2	3	4	5	6	7	8	9	10	11	12	13	14	15	16	17	18	19	20	21	22	23	24	25	26	27	28
	Menstruation													Ovulation	Luteal Phase (ovulation to menstruation)													
Ovulation Pain (Y/N)														Y (13-16)														
Contentment (H/M/L)			H							H					H							M/L						
Creativity/ Energy Level (H/M/L)			H							H																		
Hormones	Follicle-stimulating					Luteinizing Hormone / Estrogen															Progesterone							
	Inspiration; connected to others / Best time to act on ideas here														Reflection; connected to pain / Pay attention to this and give yourself time alone and time to reflect; best ideas here													
Food: Fasting (F) Overeat (O)	• To help with PMS, try either no dairy or organic dairy, limited red meat and egg yolks, no trans-fatty acids (partially hydrogenated oils), and lower re-fined carbohydrates (cookies, chips, etc.) in the latter half of the cycle (it's actually helpful to keep these habits in general)																											
	• Overall, it is good to take a multivitamin-mineral, B6 (100mg), essential fatty acids, magnesium, and Vitamin E																											
Exercise	Try to do at least twenty minutes of aerobic exercise three times each week																											
Breast Self-Exam						X																						
	1	2	3	4	5	6	7	8	9	10	11	12	13	14	15	16	17	18	19	20	21	22	23	24	25	26	27	28

All this seeks to change a negative perspective on menstruation to a positive one. Gloria Steinem's "What if Men Could Menstruate" shows the power of a changed perspective:

> So what would happen if suddenly, magically, men could menstruate and women could not? Clearly, menstruation would become an enviable, worthy, masculine event: Men would brag about how long and how much. Young boys would talk about it as the envied beginning of manhood. Gifts, religious ceremonies, family dinners, and stag parties would mark the day. To prevent monthly work loss among the powerful, Congress would fund a National Institute of Dysmenorrhea. Doctors would research little about heart attacks, from which men would be hormonally protected, but everything about cramps.[8]

Steinem suggests that if men menstruated, their perspective on menstruation would be a positive one. Thus, perhaps we women can change our negative perspective. One of the participants in *Woman* recognized the power of a changed perspective:

> Instead of seeing [menstruation]as a nuisance and disturbance to an otherwise happy life, I see it as rhythm, or cycle that brings consistency to my life. It is a reminder of my ability to give life, and I can reflect on how I have given life to others through the past month. It can also be a reminder for me to take some time by myself. By using different, more positive words I can change my perception.

"I've learned the importance of understanding my body and my period. To not ignore my monthly period but value it more and take time to process my emotional state during this time. Does it always happen? No, but it's something I wish to work on."

A woman's perspective on her sexuality and menstruation can be changed and thus free her to bless her body and inhabit it well.

Speaking of menstruation, I've often been fascinated that the Synoptic Gospels write about a woman who had been subject to bleeding for 12 years (Matt 9:18–26, Mark 5:21–40, Luke 8:40–56). I've talked to students who have continual bleeding due to polycystic ovarian syndrome, and this story speaks to their experience.

8. Steinem, "If Men Could Menstruate."

Jesus, on his way to heal a dying girl, takes time out from that rush to acknowledge the healing of a bleeding woman. She had been isolated socially, physically, and spiritually for twelve years because of her bleeding and Jesus declared her clean. He could have just rushed on to heal the dying girl, but he wanted to publicly praise the bleeding woman's faith. Jesus cared about her bleeding. Because of the fall, uterine linings do not always shed regularly, there is infertility, endometriosis, hormonal imbalance, and even more. Let us let go of any shame and face these and other life events with solidarity and support as women together. Let us embrace these factors of our sexuality!

To chat about over tea, coffee, and/or chocolate:

How do you feel about your sexuality? Do you know and understand how it all works?

How do you feel about menstruation and what do you think this chapter offers you in terms of your understanding of it?

Track your menstrual cycle using the chart on the above pages. Then chat about what you learned.

Prayer

Holy Spirit, you who are called the Comforter, I ask you to comfort me in my loneliness. Transform me into a woman that runs to you rather than to short-lived social pleasure, into a woman who loves the body that you have called good in its sexuality. Please teach me what all of this means and guide me not into temptation. Jesus, you called the people to love their neighbor as themselves, and while I seek to love others, help me to love myself. I pray all this in the name of the Father, Son, and Holy Spirit.

Amen.

7

Sexy Self-Care

Embracing Our Physicality

You start out happy that you have no hips or boobs. All of a sudden you get them, and it feels sloppy. Then just when you start liking them, they start drooping.

~ CINDY CRAWFORD, MODEL

This is a call to arms. A call to be gentle, to be forgiving, to be generous with yourself. The next time you look into the mirror, try to let go of the story line that says you're too fat or too sallow, too ashy or too old, your eyes are too small or your nose too big; just look into the mirror and see your face. When the criticism drops away, what you will see then is just you, without judgment, and that is the first step toward transforming your experience of the world.

~ OPRAH WINFREY, TALK SHOW HOST, PRODUCER, ACTOR, PHILANTHROPIST

A cultural fixation on female thinness is not an obsession about female beauty but an obsession about female obedience.

~ NAOMI WOLF, AUTHOR, SOCIAL CRITIC, POLITICAL ACTIVIST

You may be wondering why, in a spiritual book about being a woman, I am placing significant emphasis on the physical body. Are we not, as some have said, spiritual beings having a temporary physical existence? No, we aren't, not really. When God created humans as spiritual and physical it was called "very good." Our eternal future has both spiritual and physical elements to it (a resurrection body, a banqueting table, a new earth). Besides, while here on earth we cannot separate our spirituality and our physicality; we are integrated human beings who are spiritual, physical, sexual, emotional, intellectual, and more.

Our spirits are in bodies; we cannot separate body and spirit, and what we do in our bodies affects our spirits, as what we do in our spirits affects our bodies. Abusing our bodies, then, whether tangibly (e.g., eating disorders) or intangibly (e.g., calling ourselves ugly) has spiritual effects. Therefore, paying attention to one's physicality and sexuality are important *spiritual* disciplines.

This is probably most obviously illustrated by sexual intercourse, an act that unites two physical bodies in such a way that "the two become one flesh."[1] Paul even states that if one unites with a prostitute there is a similar spiritual bond and the two still become one flesh (1 Cor 6:16). This is such a strong picture that a consistent biblical analogy of the spiritual unity between God and God's children is marriage and it intimates a bond similar to sexual intercourse.[2]

The prophets illustrate spiritual disobedience and separation from God as adultery, most graphically illustrated by Hosea's life story of seeking after his prostitute wife and always being faithful to her. And the church is called the bride of Christ. The biblical witness sees sexual intercourse and marriage as not only physical, but also spiritual. Healthy sexuality influences healthy spirituality.

Physical Health and Exercise

Healthy spirituality can also be influenced by other kinds of healthy physicality as well. In the above chart about the menstrual cycle, there were healthy food recommendations as well as recommendations for exercise because what we do physically (eating well and exercising) has a positive overall effect on our menstrual cycle. If exercise and healthy eating can

1. See Gen 2:24, Matt 19:5–6, Mark 10:7–8, 1 Cor 6:16, Eph 5:31.

2. See Ezra 16, Hosea, and other passages, primarily in the prophets.

mitigate any negative impact of our menstrual cycles, can they not also impact our spiritual life? PMS symptoms include greater irritability and some women become mean and sin against others during this time. Our sin and anger, regardless of its cause, can create a spiritual distance between God and us. This distance can be overcome, but our spirituality is healthier when consistently without that distance. Proper diet and exercise can help lessen those symptoms, thus keep us feeling closer to God.

> "I really needed to learn better self-care. I hadn't really considered myself worth it. But I am realizing that as I begin to take care of myself more I am loving myself more."

As stated in chapter 2, part of the essence of the image of God in humans is that we are called to co-steward creation. That stewardship does not begin with saving the whales, but with taking care of our physical bodies, not only because of how health affects spirituality, but because we are called by God to steward our bodies. To clarify, I am not advocating that we each become a size four with tanned and toned limbs and a flat stomach. The goal is not a size; rather, the goal is *health*.

Health comes not only with eating well and exercising but also with actions like getting enough sleep. Participants in *Woman* have found, through charting their cycles, that they do not consistently get enough sleep. We all know that sleep affects our moods, which affect—well, honestly, they affect everything, even the way we relate to God. Physical health and spiritual health are thus integrally related. Author Gary Thomas writes, "For most of our lives, we have emphasized growing our souls, not always realizing that a lack of physical discipline can undercut and even erode spiritual growth."[3] Knowing ourselves involves taking care of ourselves physically. Physical self-care can have broad-reaching positive implications.

"God created bodies to *do* things—not just to be admired for their beauty."[4] And often our bodies can do more than we could even imagine. "By looking at your body as an *instrument* rather than an *ornament*, you'll find new and compelling motivation to embrace the kind of active lifestyle that fortifies your soul."[5]

---

3. Thomas, *Every Body Matters*, 12.
4. McMinn, *Growing Strong Daughters*, 119; emphasis original.
5. Thomas, *Every Body Matters*, back cover; emphasis original.

I had an active childhood, was involved in sports throughout my youth, and possibly my favorite physical activity was hiking. Thus, as an adult, when the opportunity came to hike and camp at the bottom of the Grand Canyon, I jumped at it. We were five women on this adventure, and we hiked the seven miles down to the Colorado River in the morning sun. The day before, however, we had chatted with someone who had spent two nights at the bottom of the canyon and raved about Bridal Veil Falls, a thirteen-mile-flat round-trip hike from the campground. His excitement rubbed off, and one of the other friends and I thought we were ready to do both the hike down and the hike to the falls on the same day.

We started the flat hike with a comfortable dip in a rushing stream, and continued with strength and vigor until we reached the unfortunately disappointing trickle that the man had applauded the day before. We started back, and the fatigue began to take over, especially when we realized we still had several miles to go and had run out of food and water. Having played sports, though, we knew that our bodies could do a lot more than we felt like they could, and we began to fight mentally, encouraging one another to walk fast so that we could get to the Shadow Ranch snack bar to eat a Snickers and drink lemonade. Our legs cried out in pain, but we ignored them, continued anyway, and we made it. Though it was probably unwise to attempt twenty miles in the hot desert sun, I always look back on that event as a time when the relationship with my body that began with sports helped me later in life.

Knowing one's body through physical activity has many positive effects, and it is never too late to start. In fact, statistics show that "girls who play sports do better in school, are three times more likely to graduate from high school, are 93% less likely to get involved in drugs, and are 80% less likely to get pregnant."[6] Though this proves correlation rather than causation, it does seem that physical activity also helps in other areas. I've known several women who were not active growing up, but in their adulthood, they have started running independently or taking classes like Zumba at the gym. It is never too late to take care of your body, and it's easiest when you have partners to do it with you!

---

6. McMinn, *Growing Strong Daughters*, 119. These statistics are from Renzetti and Curran's *Women, Men, and Society*, published in 1995.

Bodily Changes

> "It is so important as a woman to eat healthy, exercise, and take care of my body... I've gained the knowledge that my body will change and it won't be the same as it is now, but throughout the process of change, it is healthy to be aware of my system. Staying healthy is not only for myself, but for the sake of serving others as well."

I like some television shows that highlight the woman's experience, and before I had a DVR, I would be subjected to all the commercials that are aired for would-be viewers of such shows. Apparently, viewers like myself needed to get rid of wrinkles in various ways, dye our graying hair, and take diet pills. The message I received made me feel badly about myself.

As we think about our bodies, however, it's important to embrace the changes that come. I wrote earlier about the crisis that occurred when I was twenty-nine and teaching my first college classes, trying to figure out what a woman was. At that point, I also felt really old—thirty was coming and I had thought my life would be different than it actually was when I reached that decade. One morning, I was in front of the mirror, saw all of my gray hairs, and determined that I couldn't live with them. So, I railed against being almost thirty by getting the tweezers and pulling out every single last one. It felt good until they all started to return, one by one, kinky and sticking up straight rather than being the same texture as my other hair. By the time they returned, I was feeling more at peace with being thirty, and decided that I would let the gray come, call it moonlight, and remember the classes I taught, the mind-bending PhD study, and the students that facilitated the growth of every gray hair.

Now I am forty, and most people still can't see my gray, so I've got nothing to complain about. We all make different choices regarding our hair, none of which is any better than the other. However, even as our hair changes as we grow older, so also does our body. Pregnancy, surgeries, life stress, and other circumstances make our bodies look different. As a seminar leader recently quipped, "We all need to remember that we aren't eighteen anymore." But being eighteen isn't the best way to be. If we embrace our own story, as suggested in the "Beginnings" chapter, being fully alive *where we are* is the best way to be. The more I love myself *as I am* and continue to strive toward health—embracing my story and my bodily changes—the better my contribution to the world.

In addition, aging, asthma, cystic fibrosis, multiple sclerosis, injuries from car accidents, and many other conditions affect the ways in which we pursue health. As in the story of the bleeding woman, Jesus cares about the bodily conditions of people and often heals them, but did not heal everyone. In this fallen world, we are called to solidarity with one another as we live with or fight these conditions. We can pray and help in other tangible ways. Each person's bodily story is unique, with unique blessings and unique challenges; let us not only embrace our own story and our own body, but also encourage others.

> "I've gained a sense of confirmation that it is not only allowed but necessary for me to care for myself."

Body Image

Physical health and body image often exist hand in hand. As Jean Kilbourne's *Killing Us Softly* video series has pointed out, the media constantly bombards us with images that we consciously and subconsciously accept as portraying what we should look like, even though the bodies displayed are air-brushed, otherwise visually engineered, and often anorexic. Her videos are very informative and often shocking.[7]

> "I came to see just how common some of the struggles I have endured are. I also have come to desire embracing my sexuality, and my body just as created."

Author Lisa Bloom recently wrote about how she refuses to tell little girls how beautiful they are, even though many are incredibly cute and it's hard not to gush the truth. Rather, she chooses to talk to them about what they are interested in. She gives the following reason for her actions:

> *ABC News* reported that nearly half of all three- to six-year-old girls worry about being fat . . . 15 to 18 percent of girls under 12 now wear mascara, eyeliner and lipstick regularly; eating disorders are up and self-esteem is down; and 25 percent of young American women would rather win *America's Next Top Model* than the Nobel

7. See *Killing Us Softly* videos on YouTube and http://www.jeankilbourne.com/videos/ for more information.

Peace Prize. Even bright, successful college women say they'd rather be hot than smart. A Miami mom just died from cosmetic surgery, leaving behind two teenagers. This keeps happening, and it breaks my heart.

Teaching girls that their appearance is the first thing you notice tells them that looks are more important than anything. It sets them up for dieting at age 5 and foundation at age 11 and boob jobs at 17 and Botox at 23. As our cultural imperative for girls to be hot 24/7 has become the new normal, American women have become increasingly unhappy. What's missing? A life of meaning, a life of ideas and reading books and being valued for our thoughts and accomplishments.[8]

Unfortunately, women have become obsessed with the way we look, and respond to this obsession with many actions that can be categorized as "body obsession" or "body neglect." Michelle Graham writes about this and other body image issues from a Christian perspective in *Wanting to Be Her: Body Image Secrets Victoria Won't Tell You*. She calls for balance between body obsession (actions due to an obsession with what others think of our appearance or in order to prove our worth), and body neglect (actions that hurt or show no concern for our bodies). We should be concerned about our bodies and take care of them, but not be obsessed with how we look.

The female models we see displayed in magazines and videos are 5'9" and 110 pounds, while the average American woman is 5'4" and 142 pounds. Beautiful actresses use body doubles, 85 percent of whom have breast implants.[9] Both Graham's book and Kilbourne's documentaries easily prove that the images are altered in a variety of ways, and in real life not even the models themselves look like their magazine cover picture.

So, what's the answer? How can I love myself *and* my body *as it is* while continuing to pursue both physical and spiritual health? Like womanhood, this is a journey—the important part is being on the journey and moving forward toward a healthy body image. Often, lasting change must begin "from the inside out" rather than "from the outside in." That is, we think that external change that is not motivated by internal change will not produce lasting effects. For example, if a conflict has divided us from a close friend or family member, we want our hearts to change toward them before we are reconciled. We do not want to act as if we are reconciled before we actually feel that way. While this "from the inside out" theory

8. Bloom, "How to Talk to Little Girls."

9. McMinn, *Growing Strong Daughters*, 111.

has merit, especially in a conflict situation, it cannot be universally applied. Sometimes it's the external change that motivates the internal change. With regard to our relationship to ourselves, often changing the way we adorn our bodies without changing our bodies *at all* results in a more positive body image.

"What Not to Wear"

The television show *What Not to Wear* is a poignant example of how our tangible, visible self is related to our inner, intangible self, and how outward change causes inner change. Each show begins with a visual record of a person's bad style, and then a surprise meeting between that person, his or her friends, and Stacy and Clinton, the show's style gurus. The person agrees to receive several thousand dollars in exchange for surrendering their wardrobe to Stacy and Clinton and then shopping for clothing according to Stacy and Clinton's rules. While the premise of the show is only to change people's really bad style to good style, the participants often tearfully realize that their outward lack of style reflects their inward attitude of shame and self-hatred. The outward transformation during the show parallels the inward transformation to self-acceptance and self-love and is often a beautiful rite of passage.

Many Christian women receive conflicting messages about body image. The world teaches them to flaunt sexuality and their physical bodies, and the church teaches them to not explore sexuality until marriage. These two contradictory ideas reflect a common theme when it comes to outward adornment in particular—women dress for others rather than dressing and acting in ways that are true to their unique, individual identity. The world teaches women to dress in order to attract men, and the church teaches them to dress in a way that does "not cause a man to stumble."[10] Now, I am not suggesting that we never think about others when we adorn our bodies, but rather to think about our own true identity *more* than the unpredictable thoughts of others when we dress. Even Stacy and Clinton try to understand each participant's personality and to guide them to clothing that reflects that personality, rather than teaching them to impress others.

10. Two of the rites studied in my dissertation had statements such as this: the one written by Chuck Stecker and the True Love Waits rite. For more discussion on male/female relationships, outward adornment, and sexuality, see the sexuality section in chapter 11, "Harry Was Wrong."

Besides clothing, the two final portions of *What Not to Wear* include hair and makeup. While getting good haircuts is part of investing in yourself and we should know how to wear makeup for appropriate occasions or professional situations, balance, rather than obsession, in this area is appropriate. Allowing the natural self to shine through is good.

Sexy Science

In *Woman,* open discussions about body image are followed by a Christian *What Not to Wear* as part of the journey toward restoring a positive body image. We call it "The Science of Sexy," from Bradley Bayou's *The Science of Sexy: Dress to Fit Your Unique Figure with the Style System That Works for Every Shape and Size.* When we define "sexy," it has more to do with exuding confidence than baring one's body and inviting sexual intercourse. Again, sexuality is different from sexual intercourse. Sexuality (and sexiness) for women is to inhabit the female body well. A confident, professionally dressed woman is very sexy, since sexy has more to do with confidence than plunging necklines, short skirts, or thongs. In fact, Bayou, a couture fashion designer for celebrities, asserts that sexiness is based on balance, not bared skin. He says that the human eye is attracted to symmetry, and though most of us do not have a symmetrical body, we can dress in a way that makes our bodies look symmetrical (even symmetrical bodies can look asymmetrical according to how they are adorned).[11]

My friend watched a documentary whose name she cannot remember, but the story was of a woman who no longer felt generally "good in her own skin" or even attractive to her husband. In order to help her, friends brought her to a small hall where women of all shapes and sizes who felt "good in their own skin" sat naked. She was amazed that their confidence made any shape or size very attractive. Though she was not ready to bare her whole body, she began to recite the following mantra both when she looked at her naked self in the mirror and as she went through her days: "I am a confident, attractive woman in a very sexy body." Her body image was restored even though her body did not change; she simply changed her perspective.

The "science of sexy" involves measuring one's shoulders, waist, and hips, as well as revealing weight and height. *Woman* participants are challenged to state the above mantra and be measured by the leaders, while

11. Bayou, *The Science of Sexy,* 16–18.

listening to upbeat songs that celebrate womanhood. For some this
and for some it's nearly impossible. Bayou's *Science of Sexy* categorizes the
measurements into forty-eight different "dressing rooms," with specific
suggestions of what to wear (including jewelry, accessories, and shoes) that
will make each body appear symmetrical, teaching how to adorn each body
well. The "dressing rooms" and Bayou's other suggestions (Ten "Dress-Sexy"
Commandments, glossary, and dream closet checklist) help women have
an idea of what to look for when shopping. Following Bayou's guidelines
when choosing clothing to try on also helps maintain a positive body image
while in the dressing room. When women see themselves in clothing that
flatters them, their entire perspective on their body can change. Women
can be empowered to dress with confidence and beauty in ways that are appropriate to varying situations and show respect to themselves and others.
So, grab the book, a tape measure, some friends, and get shopping!

This outside-in change must be partnered with inside-out change to
become a positive perspective on one's body. When we dress appropriately
and well for the situations in which we find ourselves, when we positively
transform our perspective on our physical selves, our confidence and personality are enabled to shine forth, unhindered by negative body image.

Physical health and exercise, embracing our bodily changes, and
transforming our body image will all not only make us feel better physically, but also emotionally and socially. Furthermore, they will have a
positive effect on our spirituality. Not that any of this is easy—that's why
we can think of them as spiritual *disciplines*. Like reading the Bible, prayer,
or fasting, it takes hard work and determination to make habits, but the
results are worth the effort! May our physical changes become outside-in
transformation!

To chat about over tea, coffee, and/or chocolate:

How do you feel about your body physically? Do you practice self-care in
terms of nutrition and exercise? How would you like to grow in this area?

Have you noticed any bodily changes as you get older? How do you respond to them?

How healthy is your body image? Why? How would you like to grow in
this area?

Prayer

Holy Spirit, you who are called the Comforter, I ask you to comfort me in my loneliness. Transform me into a woman that runs to you rather than to short-lived social pleasure, into a woman who loves the body that you have called good, in both its sexuality and its physicality. Please teach me what all of this means and guide me not into temptation. Jesus, you called the people to love their neighbor as themselves, and while I seek to love others, help me to love myself. I pray all this in the name of the Father, Son, and Holy Spirit.

Amen.

8

Stand and Speak
Confidence and Voice

I was proud to be in America, not just because here I found my voice but because the country made me the woman I am today, a woman with a fierce voice, a woman without shame. I grew up hearing that I was stubborn, a troublemaker, hard-headed, and not good enough. But I had been wise enough to look in the mirror. I liked what I was, and I said to myself, I am worthy, lovable, and good enough.

~ SORAYA MIRE, SOMALIAN HUMAN RIGHTS ACTIVIST

I write for those women who do not speak, for those who do not have a voice because they were so terrified, because we are taught to respect fear more than ourselves. We've been taught that silence would save us, but it won't.

~ AUDRE LORDE, CARIBBEAN-AMERICAN WRITER

You gain strength, courage and confidence by every experience in which you really stop to look fear in the face. You are able to say to yourself, "I have lived through this horror. I can take the next thing that comes along." You must do the thing you think you cannot do.

~ ELEANOR ROOSEVELT, FIRST LADY, WRITER, HUMANITARIAN

ACTS 5 TELLS OF the persecution of the apostles. Because the Sadducees and the high priest were jealous of their popularity, they arrested the apostles and had them put in jail. Miraculously, the angel of the Lord frees them and instructs them, "Go, stand in the temple courts . . . and tell the people all about this new life" (5:20). Another version, the NASB, tells them to "stand and speak," as does the title of this chapter.

We women, as we have been freed from sin through Christ, and further freed through the Christian truth in this book must stand and speak to others. Though we may find ourselves dealing with much opposition, we will choose to not succumb to the "jails" in which others may place us. Let us develop our confidence and voice, and let us be those who stand and speak.

Confidence

Each topic highlighted in this section on relationship to self is integrally related to the others. As one's body image is redeemed, often one's confidence also increases. Even Stacy and Clinton have a short clip about being confident on their *What Not to Wear* website. Clinton acknowledges the elaborate concept of confidence, stating that it starts inside a person and is then shown to the world. Stacy agrees and recommends stepping away from the mirror and working on a meaningful project, learning a new skill, or seeing oneself in others' eyes. These actions help a woman understand herself and build confidence. Armed with this confidence, then, she can take responsibility for her appearance and have a style that agrees with who she really is.[1]

Confidence is primarily displayed in a woman's actions, but what she wears can display her confidence as well. One of my mentees discovered that she loved hats, and when she wore one, she walked around campus with confidence—meeting others' eyes and feeling good about herself. However, without the hat, she tended to look down and slump under the weight of her backpack. When she decided to walk in confidence even without the hat, her perspective on herself was transformed positively.

Lisa McMinn writes that a person's confidence is often shaped by the home in which they were raised. The following table illustrates this correlation:[2]

1. "On Being Confident."
2. Ideas on the table are adapted from McMinn, *Growing Strong Daughters*, 52–54.

Table 4: Confidence

CONFIDENCE		
Confidence Type	**Characteristics**	**Corresponding Home Descriptors**
Absence of Confidence	• Entirely dependent on others to direct them • Afraid of any risk • Feel incompetent and act passively	• Family did not talk about anything • Children had to simply be obedient
Listening Confidence	• Listen & learn from others; encourage others to talk • Submit without question to authority • Do not contribute to the conversation	• Home was very hierarchical, with the one in authority unquestioned
Confidence in Self	• Strong and independent • Do not trust others • Do not trust authority because authorities have hurt them	• Children were belittled and needed to obey and not question • Father was emotionally or physically absent
Confidence in Reason	• Work very hard at knowing things through reason • Afraid of appearing stupid • Speak, but only after having thoroughly thought something through	• Family was connected and caring • Family had reciprocity and mutuality
Holistic Confidence	• Integrate and evaluate what others say, subjective intuition, and the voice of reason • Make and follow through with decisions	• Family was connected and caring • Family had reciprocity and mutuality

Take a moment to locate yourself in the descriptions, and see if your home life is reflected or not. Please know that in spite of the home in which we were raised, we can move toward holistic confidence. I have. Few people who know me today would believe that in high school and college, I lacked holistic confidence, and was more apt to display listening confidence or confidence in reason. I paid attention, but was silent in class, never asking questions. I thought that at some point, the veil would drop and everyone would know how stupid I was. Still today, when I am in a seminar, I get a little nervous about asking questions and am amazed at others who seem to be able to think quickly and express themselves clearly for all to hear. The journey toward holistic confidence as I teach has been a long one, and my confidence can still vary according to the situation. However, I found that my confidence grew as I took the risk of speaking as a student in graduate classes. I discovered that others did not judge me as stupid and that my comments that were not yet completely formed could still be good comments.

Self-Talk

Sometimes, our confidence grows when we replace negative self-talk with positive self-talk. For one participant in *Woman*, this began to happen when she stated, "I am a confident, attractive woman in a very sexy body." The following is how she remembers it:

> Sitting nervously in that meeting, I could not understand why I would be pressed to say a statement that I could hardly believe to be true for myself. I was told that I'd have to say it before I could take my seat again, and so I forced it out of my mouth. It felt awkward and uncomfortable. Looking back, saying that statement was the beginning of a change in the way in which I chose to speak about myself. I had become so accustomed to speaking negativity over myself. That night, that mantra, would be the beginning of a shift in how I view myself. I learned that *I am* created beautifully, and living in that truth has been transformational for me.

Changing the ways we speak about ourselves can transform us into confident women.

One type of negative self-talk that women tend toward was picked up by a cereal company. Special K recently launched a campaign called "Fight Fat Talk," stating that 93 percent of women fat talk, or state negative ideas about their bodies. This happens especially when shopping for clothes, and it is destructive to managing their health. They created a video that portrays women shopping in a store whose clothing tags have negative "fat talk" phrases that have actually been shared on social media, including statements like, "Feeling so disgusted about my figure at the moment #Cow," and "Cellulite is in my DNA." We bully ourselves when we speak about ourselves using negative words that we would never use for others, and Special K calls for positive words to shut down fat talk.[3]

As Christians, the basis for our identity is in Christ. "I have been crucified with Christ and I no longer live, but Christ lives in me. The life I now live in the body, I live by faith in the Son of God, who loved me and gave himself for me" (Gal 2:20). "Therefore, there is now no condemnation for those who are in Christ Jesus, because through Christ Jesus the law of the Spirit who gives life has set you free from the law of sin and death" (Rom 8:1–2). Our identity is in Christ's love and self-sacrifice as well as freedom from the law of sin and death.

The oft-used phrase, "I'm just a sinner saved by grace," is one that bothers me. While it is true that we sin and that we have been saved by the grace of God through Jesus Christ, as Christians, our identity is not in our sin. Our identity is as a saint, one made holy by God. We must call ourselves saints who sometimes sin, rather than calling ourselves sinners. When we became Christians, we received a new identity, which is fleshed out in the first half of many of Paul's many letters. If you were to read the first two chapters of Ephesians, for example, you would see the contrast Paul makes between who his audience was before they knew Christ, and who they now are as Christians. The same can apply for us, and the following is a summary of that passage:

> We are not disobedient children of wrath, but we bring God pleasure as adopted children and are members of God's household. We are not dead, but we are made alive together with Christ and are seated in the heavenly places with Christ by grace. We are not hopeless strangers who are far away, but we have been brought near; we are saved; we have received peace; we have received reconciliation, and we are one. Together, we are a dwelling place for God.

Reminding ourselves of these truths daily can increase our confidence.

3. "Shhhhut Down Fat Talk."

When Neil Anderson wrote about spiritual warfare in *Victory Over the Darkness*, he made a list of characteristics that define our identity in Christ, that can be grouped under the headings "I am accepted," "I am secure," and "I am significant."[4] Among other statements, the list includes assertions about being free forever from condemnation, being made complete, and being blessed with every spiritual blessing. I remember the first time I saw the list—I couldn't believe that they were all true, so I looked up every Scripture reference. Sure enough, they were completely true, so I place a copy of the list in my Bible in order to remind myself. It is healthy to remind ourselves of the truth about our identity in Christ.

Continual meditation on positive truth makes a difference in our lives, whether it is the truth about who we are in Christ, or positive truth about who we really are as individuals. Rather than focusing on who we are not, we can make a choice to love who we are and focus on the positive. This change in focus will make us more confident. Take your thoughts captive and make them obedient to Christ (Rom 12:1–3).

Confidence comes from accepting who we are and thinking of our good characteristics as strengths. Business leader Nina DiSesa wrote the following about confidence in her career:

> When I realized that I could emulate the best male strengths without losing my female ones I became truly confident. That was my edge. Most men just don't have our strengths and they can't fake them. Most of them don't nurture, don't always listen and aren't overflowing with empathy. But empathy is the next best thing to mind reading. If you know how people feel you can deduce how they will behave and what will motivate them. That gives women an edge over men. And where you can work an edge, success will often follow.[5]

Rather than thinking that her "feminine" empathy made her weak, she changed her perspective and realized its strength.

Developing Confidence

The thing about confidence and the next topic, voice, is that they only develop through use. As I noted above, I moved out of listening confidence

---

4. Anderson, *Victory Over the Darkness*, 45–47 and 57–59. See http://www.webministries.info/papers/whoiamin.htm to access the online list that has the cited headings.

5. DiSesa, "For Career Women."

STAND AND SPEAK 97

and toward holistic confidence by speaking. Psychotherapist Maud Purcell gives several tips on becoming a more confident person, including taking risks. She writes, "If you put off taking action until you have confidence, you'll never do it. In the field of psychology we have come to understand that by changing our behavior, we can change our feelings. So if you take action, and do so with a semblance of outward confidence, the inward, true feeling of confidence, will follow."[6] Just as we concluded in the portion on body image, outward action affects inward disposition. Purcell further recommends trying new things, sticking with new challenges even when they are hard (that's what a challenge is after all, isn't it?), and implementing action plans.[7]

Purcell also recommends finding a mentor, which we mentioned in the "Beginnings" chapter as a way to ask for help. If you lack confidence, find someone with confidence who can mentor you. In addition to being mentored, emulating the examples of biblical women as described in the section on relationship with God may also increase confidence—they are fantastic examples to follow!

Oprah Winfrey has highlighted several daring role models whose habits are inspiring to me. Pat Gallant-Charette is the oldest woman to swim the Catalina Channel and the Tsugaru Strait. She finds confidence in small successes.[8] Even though her goal may have been to swim a long race, the first time she swam a mile in less than forty-five minutes was a "small success" that she celebrated. I call this "rewarding approximations," a skill I learned in elementary education. When I taught kindergarten kids to write down what they heard, and their first rendition of "cat" was "ct," I thought of that as a small success, and I rejoiced with them. They learned how to write it completely as time went on, but just writing "ct" was a success in itself, deserved reward, and gave them confidence. Rather than only looking to the accomplishment of a "big picture" goal, rewarding the small successes that lead to that goal increases confidence.

Outward actions, rewarding small successes, and positive self-talk may increase our confidence, but confidence needs a firm basis from the inside. A Christian woman's confidence is based in who she is in Christ as well as an acceptance and love of her own characteristics and life as one crafted,

6. Purcell, "The Self-Confidence Formula."

7. Ibid.

8. Winfrey, "Six Daring Women."

valued, and guided by God. As I recommended in "Beginnings," love your own life and live it well—embrace your story! This instills confidence.

Voice

While it may be inspiring to speak about how to act with confidence, you may be remembering situations that seem to have stolen your confidence from you; perhaps those are times you have been silenced. Many of those participating in *Woman* have had experiences that have taken their voice and silenced them, some of the examples being when they could not tell their story of abuse or when that story was not believed. In order to regain confidence, a woman's story of silencing must be told and her voice restored to her through empowering prayer and ensuing action. Perhaps you have trusted friends on the journey with you to whom you can tell your story and who will then empower your voice through prayer and action.

Finding Our Voice

But even when we have gotten beyond past silencing or have never struggled with it, most women still face difficulties in finding our voice and using it. Some are afraid of having a weak voice or no voice at all. Others are afraid of having a shrill, annoying, or bossy voice. This is not simply about tone, but also about the deep inner perspective that is shown as we speak. So often, rather than risking an unliked or unaccepted voice, we silence ourselves.

A researcher on woman's voice, Jane Stephens, states, "[Voice] begins with one's ability to own oneself, and it grows with one's ability to give that self to the world. It thrives at the cusp of those two experiences."[9] Owning myself and giving myself to the world—that's vulnerable. I have to believe that who I am is good and that I have something to give, regardless of how others respond.

As a professor, I speak a lot, and I know what it feels like to fully find my voice as I speak in front of people. It happens when I am unencumbered by self-doubt, I have a platform, and I am able to flow from thought to thought. It's as if there's a river from God flowing through me and out to others. Everything is aligned, all is in sync, and it feels amazingly anointed

9. Stephens, "Voice," 185.

with Holy Spirit power! I also find my voice in personal conversation, often when I orally process an event or thought, not knowing the outcome but following the process freely to wherever it takes me. Stephens aptly describes it: "Something provokes or engages us; a door gets opened and suddenly we begin to talk. Not small talk or business talk or chitchat, but real talk about things we've discovered, observed, and considered. The power of our own voice surprises us. Something has been turned on. We are now working and thinking in a faster, fuller way."[10] I wish I could have this voice at all times, but I don't.

Most sermons that we hear in evangelical contexts are based on relatively short scriptural passages, have one "big idea," three points, and a specific application. Preachers are taught this format in seminary, and it has proven to be an effective way of communicating. This, then, is often the way I preach, especially when assigned a biblical passage. My best voice, however, comes across in first-person narrative sermons. I research a character of Scripture deeply and tell the story as if it's my own. When I write the manuscript and when I preach, I feel the same way I've described above—it flows so easily. When invited as a guest preacher, however, I always wonder whether it will be accepted, even though Jesus used stories all the time to teach. Should I do what everyone else does or should I be different? How will the difference be viewed?

When searching for her voice, pastor, author, and teacher Nancy Beach was encouraged "to avoid copying the voices of others, and instead, to zealously pursue and develop [her] own unique voice."[11] For, if we are always seeking to follow another accepted pattern of speaking (often a masculine one), we are in danger of becoming what Gloria Steinem calls "female impersonators."[12]

Carol Gilligan's work *In a Different Voice* points out that in the past what was measured as the "norm" was actually the male voice and male way of knowing and developing. Her work seeks to empower women to have a different voice from what has been erroneously assumed to be the "norm." Even as I am writing this book, I have encountered other books that are fantastic and wondered how I could say something that was even half as impactful as what they've already said. I have to keep encouraging myself with the truth that my voice is neither better nor worse. It is simply

10. Ibid., 187.

11. Beach, *Gifted to Lead*, 106.

12. Stephens, as quoted in ibid., 107.

different, and all voices are necessary. When we choose to emulate someone else's voice, when we choose not to use our voices, we are depriving the world of our true voice and calling. Everyone misses out when we are silent. Voice has advantages for us, too, for "To have voice is to be fully present, to feel counted in, and counted on, to have something to say, and to be heard."[13]

Lisa McMinn uses a striking example of what happens when women's voices aren't heard. She pictures a panel with invited experts who were specifically chosen to talk about ethical issues related to stem cell research. If only half of them are allowed to speak, the final recommendation may (likely) not be the best. The same occurs if the voice of half of God's image-bearers (women) remains silent.[14] God has created us with something to offer the world through our voices.

Using Our Voice

Sometimes, we want to be *sure* before we use our voice, but voice is not about certainty.[15] We can use our voices to engage in real talk whether or not we are certain about the entirety of what we are saying. Our voice must reveal our soul and be true to our core values in order to be authentic.[16] "Real voice is not particularly loud. A pushy voice with a sharp edge is usually just as false as the whiny voice or the one that constantly apologizes for itself."[17] The goal of using our true voice is not to persuade others, though that may be the result. It is primarily to be true to ourselves and authentic in our interaction with others.

Our voice is often what displays the image of God in us in both its relational essence as well as its stewardship over creation. While women tend to find it easier to use their authentic voice in relational contexts, we often give up our voice when called to stewardship. The first chapter referred to this description of the distortion of our call to stewardship: "In the boardroom, she disagrees with the decision for a good reason, but is silent because her relationships with those around the table are threatened by her disagreement with them." Nancy Beach encourages leading women to

13. Stephens, "Voice," 186.
14. McMinn, *Growing Strong Daughters,* 97.
15. Stephens, "Voice," 187.
16. Ibid., 191.
17. Ibid.

"develop the skill of talking back—the ability to present an alternative view, challenge the status quo, and to exert one's own unique voice."[18]

This is not the "talking back" that parents prohibit in their households. The parent-child relationship is hierarchical, but as we become adults, we interact with other men and women with whom we share the image of God equally, though we may be in differing roles. Because our perspective is different, we can offer an alternative view in our own voice, whether or not it is accepted or followed. This "talking back" is simply the ability to state an opinion that does not agree.

The reasons that I hesitate to "talk back" include the false belief that my thoughts are not valuable and the fear that I will be disappointed if others do not follow or agree with what I say. To encourage myself, I remember the prophet Ezekiel. God called him to speak God's message to a people who would not listen. God said that if he did not speak, Ezekiel would be responsible for their disobedience, but if he did speak, the people themselves would shoulder that responsibility. All Ezekiel had to do was speak—he was not responsible for others' response to his words. God has given us a voice to use for God's glory, and we are not responsible for how others respond; we are simply called to speak. The goal is to have a dialogue, not to get others to agree with us.[19]

Truth is, though, authentic voice only comes out through practice. It's not always beautiful on the first try. Often, it begins to emerge in casual, normal conversation as we seek to use our own authentic voice rather than speaking what others want us to say. It comes through our own reflection on how we used our voice as well as through truly listening to and being fully present to others.[20] It comes. It may come haltingly, or in bursts, or slowly, but it comes. And the world is better for hearing, as we are for speaking.

Beginning to develop our voices can be very simple. One of my mentees realized that she hardly used her voice in public. Since she was a student, I encouraged her to use her voice in simple situations in the classroom. For example, when there is was opportunity to read something in class, she could volunteer to read it. That action could make her accustomed to hearing her own physical voice in a public context; such an

18. Beach, *Gifted to Lead,* 115.

19. McMinn, *Growing Strong Daughters,* 98–99.

20. Nancy Beach offers several helpful hints on developing voice in normal conversation and analyzing it afterward (*Gifted to Lead,* 108–9).

action could encourage use of her authentic voice in the future because the "silence sphere"[21] had already been broken.

Perhaps you've never realized that Scripture includes the voices of women. Their voices are excellent examples to be emulated, for they bring praise to God with gusto! Miriam, Deborah, Hannah, and Mary all sing or pray strong words to God (Exod 15:20–21, Judg 5, 1 Sam 2, Luke 1:46–55), and many other words of women are recorded. As you read Scripture, note the voices of women as well as their actions. These women spoke not only to other women, but their voices also resonated to the broader population and to all future readers of Scripture. They are examples for us to follow as we begin to develop our true voice.

> Real voice is the experience of speaking and *not* leaving. Of saying what we know and feeling it ring true all the way down to our shoes, and continuing to stand in them. Of feeling strong as we stand and hearing the words and meanings that come back to us as we're standing strong in our own voice.[22]

Though others may not agree with us when we express an alternative view, we can stand strong with our biblical foremothers as well as many other women whose words have changed the world.

Now back to the mentee whose story began this section. She came back with the two lists, and her confidence grew as she stated what she liked about herself and what she loved to do. The light in her eyes and the upturn of her mouth were beautiful. She had even told her mother about the assignment and her mother wrote a list of all the things she liked about her daughter—an action that led to greater vitality in their relationship. She sat up straighter in the chair across from me, and her mother later emailed me, "[Woman] may be the single most important and valuable benefit of her education at Nyack."

The joyous, unpredictable part of the story is that the guy who had broken her heart came to visit me in my office not long ago, and thanked me for mentoring her, though I had never mentioned my relationship with her to him. He saw a completely different woman than the one he had seen before. And a year later, they returned to a romantic relationship and are now engaged to be married. Knowing herself as a woman prepared her for that life step.

21. McMinn uses this phrase in *Growing Strong Daughters,* 96–105.

22. Stephens, as quoted in Beach, *Gifted to Lead,* 117; emphasis original.

But even if she were not taking that life step, knowing herself as a woman transformed her and transforms us. Developing our relationship with ourselves means becoming women who stop avoiding loneliness but begin to embrace it and allow it to lead us to God. We can choose to call "good" what God calls good, including our physical bodies and our sexuality. We can pay attention to our cycles and our bodily changes and celebrate them all! And then we can move ahead with holistic confidence, discovering and using our own unique voice. May the Holy Spirit guide us and empower us on this journey!

To chat about over tea, coffee, and/or chocolate:

Where do you categorize yourself in terms of confidence (see the chart above)? How would you like to grow in this area?

Do you believe you have a voice? What is it like? How do you use it? How would you like to use it?

Prayer

Holy Spirit, you who are called the Comforter, I ask you to comfort me in my loneliness. Transform me into a woman that runs to you rather than to short-lived social pleasure, into a woman who loves the body that you have called good, in both its sexuality and its physicality. Please teach me what all of this means and guide me not into temptation. Remind me of who I am in Christ, build up my confidence, and help me to be faithful when I have opportunities to use my voice. Jesus, you called the people to love their neighbor as themselves, and while I seek to love others, help me to love myself. I pray all this in the name of the Father, Son, and Holy Spirit.

Amen.

SECTION THREE

Relationship with Others

"I learned the importance of having a deeper relationship with my mom to understand why she raised me a certain way."

"Mentoring has hands down been one of the greatest highlights in my womanhood journey. I value the mentor/mentee relationship significantly. I learned that my mentor and I share so many things in common and that she is a woman full of wisdom, guidance, love, and encouragement . . . . She helped me see the potential and gifts that I have and to believe and walk in confidence in them. Sometimes it is difficult to share the honest truth, but it is indeed healthy and worth it. Mentors are there to support you in both the ups and downs of life. She showed me that I can be strong and beautiful at the same time."

"I noticed so many of my struggles were shared with my peers. I now understand the importance of having a community of women that support one another."

Introduction

Created for Community

"Blessed women of God, you have come to develop your relationship with others. You have already journeyed with various people thus far, and now we journey together, investigating the positive influences in our heritage, creating healthy relationships with both sexes, pursuing social justice, spreading the gospel of Jesus Christ, maintaining sexual purity, and investigating the freedom and equality the Gospel offers to women. We welcome you."

TO ONE DEGREE OR another, we have all experienced the truth that relationships in our world are broken. The brokenness touches even the healthiest of families and completely destroys the unhealthiest. Many of us aren't far along in years when we experience betrayal, anger, hurt, and the ending of relationships. Others have not so much experienced the ending of relationships as the lack of them—some of us never know our father or mother.

And yet, we always come back to each other, don't we? Except in the bitterest of cases, we still want relationships with one another, and we still take the risks of brokenness. Inherent in us is the desire for relationship, a belief in others, and a hope for wholeness in this broken world.

When we think of Eden, we think of perfection, beauty, peace—a place we would love to stay forever. I wonder, if we could make it past the guarding cherubim and see it, whether Eden would be marred by the fall.

What's interesting and often overlooked about Eden is that before the fall, there was something wrong there. The only "not good" element was that 'adam was alone. So God solved that problem. And since that time, we are all born into relationship—daughter, son, sister, brother—relationships are embedded in our identity. Although we often use the word *relationship* to signify a dating relationship, for the purposes of this section, the word *relationship* will be generalized to denote any relationship, and specific types of relationships will be specified.

The desire for relationship reflects our creation in the image of God. As stated earlier, being in the image of God means we are created to steward the earth and we are intrinsically social, as God is. Speaker and author Ruth Haley Barton puts it well when she writes, "The God who exists as a community of equals . . . recognized that it was not good for the man to have as his only companions the animals he had been given the responsibility to oversee. Even Adam's relationship with his Creator could not provide the experience of community that comes when two or more peers commit themselves to share the journey together."[1]

Barton tells the story of Sunday afternoon meals at her home, when she often ended up in the kitchen washing dishes, though she would rather be out with the men in the living room, entering into the discussion about "life, faith and kingdom work."[2] She states that her desire for this "was really the hunger to live and work as God intended—in a community with my brothers. The creation of humankind in two sexes was intended to reflect God's eternal existence in community . . . . *Two individuals who were exactly the same could not adequately form the community that would show us who God is. It would take maleness and femaleness together to fully round out the image.*"[3] Barton's book is about men and women partnering in all areas of life, so her focus here is on the two sexes. Diversity, however, is not only *between* the two sexes but also *among* those who are of the same sex. All women are not the same, nor are all men. This diversity, this difference, reflects who God is in God's diversity.

"It is not good for the man to be alone" (Gen 2:18) does not mean that we were necessarily all created to find one other person to "complete" us. A better understanding would be that it is not good when we are not part of a community. We are created to *be* family and friends and to *need* family and friends. Happily married women admit that their husband does not complete them; he partners with them and loves them, but they need other

---

1. Barton, *Equal to the Task*, 21.
2. Ibid.
3. Ibid., emphasis added.

friends and companions along the way of life. One of the "basics" of our relationship with God includes being part of the community of Christians.

And in that community of Christians, as well as in our broader community, we may have relationships with others described as daughter, sister, friend, employee, boss, girlfriend, wife, mother, and even more. And it is good to be in relationship with people who are different from us—whether they are of the opposite sex, have different interests, or are from a different background or culture; relationships with others enrich our journey of womanhood.

Being a true part of a community requires a giving of oneself, a telling of one's story; it requires vulnerability and commitment if it is going to function well. Jean Vanier, who works with intellectually and developmentally challenged adults, writes, "It is my hope that each one of you may experience the incredible gift of friendship with people who are poor and weak, that you too, may receive life from them. For they call us to love, to communion, to compassion and to community."[4] Christians use "Communion" to describe the meal of bread and wine that Jesus offers us, connoting that we are eating together as a community. In the early church, it would be a full meal, not just bread and wine. In Middle Eastern culture, then as well as now, eating with others is an event that lasts, not a quick hello-and-goodbye, and it signifies friendship, sharing, and peace. We try to reflect that with our word, Communion.

Vanier elaborates on the word, "To be in communion means to *be with* someone and to discover that we actually belong together . . . . To be in communion with someone also means to *walk with* them."[5] To be with, to belong, to walk the journey of life with others—that's community. We desire that, and though our community is broken in places, we can choose to concentrate on the areas where it is whole, and continue to give ourselves to it.

Women tend to give ourselves to relationships more than men. Psychologist and author Dr. Harriet Lerner states that women are experts on intimate relationships, and traces this to the fact that those in subordinate positions (for reasons of gender or ethnicity) "possess a far greater understanding of the dominant group members and their culture than vice-versa."[6] Despite the fact that women's expertise on relationships derives

4. Vanier, *From Brokenness to Community*, 10.

5. Ibid., 16; emphasis original.

6. Lerner, *The Dance of Intimacy*, 6.

from a subordinate status, "the valuing of intimacy and attachments is an asset, not a liability. Surely, women's commitment to relationships is part of our proud legacy and strength."[7] We women can be satisfied that our drive for intimate relationships and community is a good desire, for it is a way we reflect our creation in the image of God.

This section, "Relationship with Others," has four different chapters. The first focuses on the basics of being in healthy relationship, including bringing your full self to others, being like Jesus in relationships, and moving toward interdependence rather than being overly independent or dependent. The next two look at relationships with the two sexes, first women, and then men. After a chapter on enjoying singleness, we focus on dating and how to do it well. May our relationships with others be renewed by what we read here!

7. Ibid., 7.

9

Relationally Healthy

Principles for the Journey

One's life has value so long as one attributes value to the life of others, by means of love, friendship, and compassion.

~ SIMONE DE BEAUVOIR, FRENCH EXISTENTIALIST

In your relationships with one another, have the same mind-set as Christ Jesus: Who, being in very nature God, did not consider equality with God something to be used to his own advantage; rather, he made himself nothing by taking the very nature of a servant, being made in human likeness. And being found in appearance as a man, he humbled himself by becoming obedient to death— even death on a cross! Therefore God exalted him to the highest place and gave him the name that is above every name, that at the name of Jesus every knee should bow, in heaven and on earth and under the earth, and every tongue acknowledge that Jesus Christ is Lord, to the glory of God the Father.

~ SAINT PAUL, PHILIPPIANS 2:5–11

HAVE YOU EVER EXPERIENCED an unhealthy relationship?

Perhaps that's a silly question. Is it part of the human condition to not only experience broken relationships but also to experience unhealthy ones? I know it's part of *my* human condition. Has it been part of yours?

Sometimes the unhealthiness comes from me and sometimes from the other person. I know I've been guilty of compromising my true self in friendships or being overly dependent, at the very least. Relationships are hard work, and at times we're tempted to quit when healthy interdependence seems unattainable and we lose our authentic selves. Even in the discouragement, though, we still think relationships are worthwhile and hang on tightly to the healthy, life-giving ones. Habits that will help us maintain healthier relationships include knowing ourselves and bringing her to others, being like Jesus in relationships, being interdependent, and learning love languages.

Know Yourself and Bring Her to Others

Lerner warns us that a woman's drive and talent for relationships is sometimes distorted. "The problem arises . . . when we confuse intimacy with winning approval, when we look to intimate relationships as our sole source of self-esteem, and when we enter relationships at the expense of the self."[1] Self-knowledge is vital for healthy relationships; we sought to develop our self-understanding in the last section, so the question now is, *how do we bring our authentic selves to our relationships?*

First, it is important to remember that our authentic self is in the image of God. We saw that women sometimes distort our reflection of the image of God by preserving our relationships at the expense of exercising our rightful rule. Thus, when we bring ourselves to others we must seek to reflect both aspects of God's image—relationality and stewardship—in balance. This takes practice.

Even in the marriage relationship when the "two become one," they are still two separate people. I remember that the minister who performed my sister's wedding had the bride and groom light the unity candle but keep their own candles lit rather than blowing them out. This visibly represented the fact that though one, they were still individuals. Vanier writes, "In a relationship of communion, you are you and I am I; I have my identity and you have yours. I must be myself and you must be yourself. We are called to grow together, each one becoming more fully himself or herself . . . . It entails deep listening to others, helping them to become more fully themselves."[2] To be fully ourselves in relationship takes time—it's part of the *process* of intimacy, for intimacy is not immediate, no matter how much we'd like it to be.

1. Lerner, *The Dance of Intimacy*, 7.
2. Vanier, *From Brokenness to Community*, 17.

I had just graduated from college when I lived in Paraguay, and I was desirous of a relationship with a man. A good friend gave me some advice about the process of intimacy that really "stuck." She said that when we meet someone we really like, we want to give him everything—all that we have and are. It's like we want to give away our whole bank account. She recommended, rather than giving him the whole account, to write a five-dollar check. If he proved faithful and trustworthy with that amount, we could write him another. The whole bank account was ours to reserve for later.[3]

Though this advice was for male-female relationships, I think it applies to all relationships. Sometimes we are so lonely and so deeply want someone else to fully walk with us in our lives that we give too much too soon. It would be better to enjoy the process of getting to know others, so that what is precious about us is revealed gradually as trust increases.

We have all likely experienced relationships that become too intense or too distant at times. Reasons for this can include one party sharing something too deep for the other party to absorb, one party demanding more than the other can give, or an unhealthy codependence. In order to avoid extreme intensity and extreme distance, one must come to the relationship as a "clear, whole, and separate 'I.'"[4] As whole persons, we look to no one else for completion; we look to others simply for companionship and help along the way.

In the same way that intimacy is a process, being a "clear, whole, and separate 'I'" is not static, but also a process. It is often in relationships that we realize heretofore unnoticed aspects of ourselves. Many of us attribute certain relationships with the healing of "holes" in our psyche, and can even remember how conflicts in a relationship or the ending of a relationship made us cognizant of personal issues and/or strengths. Because I had a distant father figure, I can remember several friendships with older men that helped heal that "hole" in my psyche. Though I am no longer in close relationship with them, I always remember their part in my healing. In none of those relationships did I become overly dependent, but I sought to work on myself as I continued in the relationship.

3. The bank account analogy is useful, but when it is drawn out to its conclusion, it fails. Even when we share all of who we are, we still "own" who we are—we don't lose it as we would if we gave someone a check for the entire account.

4. Lerner, *The Dance of Intimacy*, 18.

And that is what Lerner recommends. She emphasizes, *"Real closeness occurs most reliably not when it is pursued or demanded in a relationship, but when both individuals work consistently on their own selves."*[5] We all want to experience real closeness and intimacy—the kind that satisfies our soul's desire for connection. I can remember times when I have demanded it of others. During a particularly lonely time period, I remember expressing to a friend how much time I wanted her to spend with me. Though we were already close, she was unable to give me that kind of time and it put a strain on our relationship. I was demanding that she fill a space that she couldn't fill; I needed to work on my own self rather than fleeing aloneness.

I also remember a time when I expressed a desire—not an expectation—of greater intimacy, and it enhanced a friendship. I have very few friends from childhood, but there is one I remember meeting when I was six. Our relationship deepened and continued through sleepovers, birthday parties, many middle-school and high-school crushes on boys in the youth group, camp, and other varied activities.

As adults, we lived far apart, but still sought to keep in communication by phone. I was living alone in downtown Nyack, working through some personal issues, and realized that I was dissatisfied with our friendship. Though we loved each other deeply, our phone calls and emails were brief and sporadic. However, I realized that she was the kind of person with whom I shared significant history, I respected, and with whom I wanted to have more of a dependable relationship. I remember where I was standing as I held the phone and expressed that I felt like our relationship was undependable, she was important to me, and I wanted to be more consistent and deep with her. I added that if that wasn't what she wanted or was able to give, it was fine, but I wanted her to know what I wanted. I came to her in honesty and vulnerability, and rather than demand, I told her about myself. I was bringing my true, full self to this long-standing relationship. We both look back on that time affectionately as a turning point in our friendship— we enjoy almost weekly phone calls that last at least an hour (but could easily go much longer), and we have journeyed together through dating relationships, breakups, engagement, marriage, and so much more! In this case, I defined who "I" was and what I wanted, but I did not *demand* that she respond in only one way, giving her freedom to be herself. I was working on myself and clarifying my values as I continued in the relationship.

5. Ibid., 68; emphasis original.

Lerner has a helpful definition of working on oneself. "By 'working on the self,' I do not mean that we should maintain a single-minded focus on self-actualization, self-enhancement, or career advancement. These are male-defined notions of selfhood that we would do well to challenge. Working on the self includes clarifying beliefs, values, and life goals, staying responsibly connected to persons on one's own family tree, defining the 'I' in key relationships, and addressing important emotional issues when they arise."[6] This definition is helpful, and expands what we discussed in our last section. It is important to realize that working on oneself is a continual, never-ending process. Not only is it good for each of us as individuals, but it is key for all our relationships. "Only through our connectedness to others can we really know and enhance the self. And only through working on the self can we begin to enhance our connectedness to others."[7] May we be those who continue to grow as persons as we know ourself and bring her to others!

Be Like Jesus in Relationships

The Gospels show Jesus as a full and whole "I" who brings himself to his relationships. We already mentioned the fact that Jesus has healthy friendships with women as well as men. Barton describes his intimate relationships with women: "The intimate nature of their relationships is evidenced by strong give-and-take in conversation (see especially Christ's conversation with Mary and Martha regarding Lazarus's death in John 11), the sharing of emotion and tears (John 11:28–36), the freedom to share physical touch (John 12:1–8) and closeness (Luke 10:39), and a mutual desire to seek each other out in groups and in one-to-one interactions."[8] The Gospels have many instances that show Jesus as an example to follow in our relationships.[9]

Jesus is not one to "climb the social ladder"—no, he chooses to associate with the lowly and powerless rather than with the rich and powerful.

6. Ibid., 68–69.

7. Ibid., 9.

8. Barton, *Equal to the Task,* 196–97.

9. Women of Influence published the Bible Study manual *Radical Relationships* in 1992. It examines Jesus' relational actions that seem radical to his culture or to readers, and encourages participants to act in relationships the same way he did. Many of the cited biblical passages that follow are also cited in this text.

His discussion with the Samaritan woman at the well in John 4, for example, is a chat with one of the most marginalized people in society. And through his conversation with her, she is shown to be a woman of influence who evangelizes much of her town. Jesus' twelve disciples are not the influential Pharisees, but are primarily fishermen, of the common people. Not only does Jesus have a despised tax collector in his inner group, but he is also known to be a "friend of tax collectors and sinners" (Matt 11:19). In fact, the women in his group of disciples may have been more influential in society than the men, since the women supported his ministry financially (Luke 8:3). Jesus is not afraid to befriend the lowly and despised people; in fact, he seemed to prefer them over the lofty and lauded. To be like Jesus in our relationships, we must be courageous enough to befriend those who are often overlooked.

Jesus not only seeks relationship with those who seem to have no power, but he also encourages people to "Love your enemies and pray for those who persecute you, so that you may be children of your Father in heaven. . . . For if you love those who love you, what reward do you have? Do not even the tax collectors do the same?" (Matt 5:44–46, NRSV). He embodies this admonition on the cross when he says, "Father, forgive them, for they do not know what they are doing" (Luke 23:34). Jesus prayed for those who were crucifying him! To be like Jesus in our relationships, we must love and pray for our enemies, even if it is done from afar and they never know.

And when Jesus has a friend who doubts and questions him, he has compassion for him and helps him. Though he had heard that Jesus was alive, Thomas doubts it and demands to see and touch his wounds. Jesus shows himself to Thomas kindly but also corrects him by saying that those who do not see and yet believe are blessed (John 20:24-31). Even in his kindness and compassion, Jesus corrects others and encourages them to greater faith.

John 8 is not in the earliest manuscripts of John, but it is one of our favorite stories of Jesus—the one when he challenges the crowd to be the first to throw the stone at the woman caught in adultery, saying, "Let anyone among you who is without sin be the first to throw the stone at her" (John 8:7, NRSV). Jesus lets the people condemn themselves, has compassion on the woman, and challenges her to "go and sin no more" (verse 11). There are numerous other examples of Jesus correcting and challenging others, while still balancing the correction with kindness and compassion. Though none of these habits is easy to emulate, to balance compassion and challenge like Jesus in his relationships is perhaps the most difficult. Many women tend toward more compassion than challenge, yet balance is the goal.

Jesus seems to understand and share life with many in Scripture, empathizing with them in shame or grief, and lifting them up from their broken state. When the woman who had been bleeding for twelve years touches him and is healed, Jesus singles her out, knowing that this bleeding had brought her shame and ostracism for a long time. He brings her out of her shame and gives her dignity by commending her faith (Mark 5:21–34). Jesus also shares Mary and Martha's grief over the death of Lazarus—he is not above or outside of our suffering, but shares it with us, for Jesus weeps (John 11:35). And then he raises Lazarus from the dead and they celebrate together. We also can empathize with others, *walking with* them in their pain and joy, and thus be like Jesus in relationships.

A Women of Influence Bible study summarizes this and more of what Jesus did. He "treated women with respect and dignity, associated with people of low social standing, treated people with compassion when they expected condemnation, redefined power in personal and professional relationships, issued stern warnings on the effects of greed on our relationships with God and others, [and] outlined a revolutionary strategy for dealing with conflict."[10] Though the famed, "WWJD" does not always apply,[11] it does apply to these actions within relationships. Jesus' relationships were accomplished not in his divinity, but in his Holy Spirit anointed humanity, so we are free and empowered to follow him in these actions.

> "I have gained a love for being part of a community of women who study the Word and fellowship together."

Be Interdependent

Jesus also acts interdependently with the Father and Holy Spirit. The Trinity sets an example for us to live lives of interdependence with others, but the idea of *inter*dependence and its healthy opposition to dependence and independence may seem strange to us. "As a culture, we don't do interdependence very well. Ours is a culture whose narratives include concepts

10. MacLeod, Johnson, and Pain, *Radical Relationships*, 3.

11. Jesus would act in many ways that are not applicable to us; for example, he provided atonement for humankind and claimed to be God.

such as 'rugged individualism,' 'pull yourself up by your bootstraps' and 'every man (or woman?) for himself.' Heck, one of our national cornerstones is a document titled the Declaration of Independence."[12] Instead of interdependence, I think I've prized independence for much of my life. In fact, there were many days that I turned up the volume on the stereo to dance and sing to Ne-Yo's praise for "Miss Independent." He found something amazing and extremely attractive about a woman who could do everything on her own and wanted a man without needing him.[13] This was the kind of woman I felt like I was for many years, and Ne-Yo praised it, while in the real world, my independence isolated me. One of the disciplines I hope you have engaged, as encouraged in the "Beginnings" chapter, is asking for help, an act of interdependence. While I can identify with "Miss Independent" in that I want but don't need people, can pay my bills, and can take care of myself, I have learned that acting interdependently is a much easier and more enjoyable life.

First, it is important to understand that God is interdependent. No one person of the Trinity acts without the inclusion and support of the others; the Trinity works together as a triunity of coequal and coeternal persons.[14] The fact that we are created in the image of God reminds us that we are created for this type of interdependence. "When the Trinity is the pattern for our human communion in the church, interdependence multiplies our ability to fulfill God's purposes."[15]

However, as we know, the image of God in us has been marred by the fall. "One result [of the fall]is that men tend to become overly independent and domineering, and women overly dependent and passive."[16] Unfortunately, some believe that men *should* actually be independent and women *should* be dependent. After all, does Genesis 3:16 not record God stating to the woman, "Your desire will be for your husband, and he will rule over you"? McMinn explains,

> God was *not* setting forth a plan where men should have domin-
> ion over women, but stating a consequence of brokenness. Women
> would desire the intimacy of equals in a lifetime partnership with
> their husbands—an intimacy borne over time when two people

12. Dixon, "It's all about Interdependence."

13. Eriksen, Hermansen, and Smith, "Miss Independent."

14. "An Evangelical Statement on the Trinity."

15. Butin, *The Trinity*, 106.

16. McMinn, *Growing Strong*, 78.

mutually support, encourage, protect, and help each other. But women would not easily experience this intimacy because men would tend to rule over them as masters instead of ruling with them as partners. After the fall, the shared sense of interdependence for the task given men and women by God was distorted; this has led to a tradition where men are encouraged to be dominant and women to be passive and dependent.[17]

"Your desire will be for your husband, and he will rule over you" describes the pain of the hierarchy brought about by the first humans' disobedience to God. Women and men were created to be interdependent, not for her to desire him and for him to rule over her; it is a sinful hierarchy.

Many of us have been raised in environments that encourage either independence or dependence. A friend of mine grew up in an abusive home. She watched her mother, for years, submit to verbal and sometimes physical abuse because her understanding of being a wife required that kind of submission. The girl, naturally independent and feisty, was confused about her female identity because she knew she could not be that kind of a woman. When she was thirteen, her mother began to take a stand against the abuse, and this offered relief to the daughter. However, though raised in a home where the woman tended toward dependence and passivity, the daughter's life exhibited significant independence, and she has had to learn to be interdependent. I know of women whose circumstances have forced them to become independent adults at very young ages, and because of others' failures, have trouble depending on anyone. And still there are others who were coddled and live lives of extreme dependence on their families. They are afraid to try new things and only feel secure when they think of a dependent future.

I am not saying that any types of independence or dependence are necessarily bad or evil; rather, we would do well to avoid extreme independence and extreme dependence, and to primarily seek to be interdependent women. The table below explains these three categories and is helpful for greater understanding:[18]

17. Ibid., 80; emphasis added.
18. The definitions for the table are from McMinn, *Growing Strong Daughters*, 78–85.

Table 5: Interdependence

Descriptors of Women in These Categories		
Extremely Dependent	Extremely Independent	Interdependent
• Passive, waiting to be "saved" • Allow another (or others) to make all the decisions • Uninformed in many areas (possibly including finances, politics, car maintenance, problem-solving, etc.)	• Self-seeking; "I don't need anyone" attitude • Afraid of intimacy; afraid to trust others • Sometimes have an extreme reaction to the passivity they find unattractive • Sometimes become "like a man" in order to "make it" in a man's world	• Appropriately depend on others and are depended on by others • Able to function in areas of personal strength and allow others to fill in the gaps of weakness; learns what is necessary from others in weak areas • Able to solve problems with help from others • Committed to others' growth as well as personal growth

Take a moment to look at the chart, see where you fit, and come up with an action plan that will bring about greater interdependence in your life.

Even as we work toward becoming healthy, interdependent people, let us remember that women in Scripture, married and single, acted boldly. Deborah led the army, Huldah prophesied to the leaders, Rebekah easily left her family (Gen 24:54–61), Phoebe took Paul's letter to Rome (Rom 16:1–2), Lydia was the first European convert and housed Paul and Silas (Acts 16:11–14); there are many other examples. They were interdependent, and the interdependence included bold acts of obedience to God.

Know Your and Others' Love Language

As we seek interdependence, we must have a healthy understanding of what we desire or need in a relationship as well as what others desire or need. When our needs are met by one another interdependently, we can faithfully fulfill our chosen roles in the home, church, and society well. Our emotional needs can be called a "love tank," and when our tank is empty, it makes it hard for us to function well in the world. So how can we seek to meet others' emotional needs as well as our own?

Gary Chapman has authored numerous books that explain five love languages in many different arenas. From friendship to marriage, children to teenagers, the military to the workplace, he has proliferated his idea that each of us has a primary love language. It is the way we best feel loved, and the primary way we give love to others (though these two may be different). As our friends or partners learn to give us love in the way that we prefer to receive it, we are empowered. As we seek to love others through their preferred love language, we empower others.

Chapman divides the love languages into five categories: Words of Affirmation, Quality Time, Receiving Gifts, Acts of Service, and Physical Touch.[19] Words of affirmation include verbal compliments, encouraging words, kind words, and humble words. When he describes Quality Time, he means "giving someone your undivided attention. I don't mean sitting on the couch watching television together,"[20] but rather listening and talking, as well as engaging in quality activities together. Also, gifts are visual symbols of love, including even the gift of self or one's presence; some people's primary love language is Receiving Gifts. Acts of Service include any kind of helping another person, usually in a physical, tangible manner.

The final love language is Physical Touch, and is often misunderstood by married couples. Some think it is only sex, but it encompasses other kinds of touch that may be more important than sex. We all need to be hugged, some more than others, and when we are going through a particularly hard time, it is good for others to hold our hands. And some people, in simple interactions, are always reaching out to touch another's arm or back.

These love languages are useful in our relationships, and you can visit http://www.5lovelanguages.com/profile/ to take a quick survey and learn your primary love language as well as to understand others' love languages

19. Chapman, *The Five Love Languages*.
20. Ibid., 59.

better. As interdependent actors, we can help others feel loved and figure out how to feel loved ourselves so that our "love tank" is full and overflows!

We have been created for community because we reflect the image of God and it is not good for us to be alone. Scripture states that God "sets the lonely in families" (Psalm 68:6), giving us opportunity to act interdependently and to belong. When we know ourselves and bring her to others, we can have healthy relationships and follow the many examples of how Jesus related to others. The love languages act as a helpful tool alongside all of this.

And yet, we cannot forget that relating to others is a holy, godly act, not to be taken lightly. We, as image-bearers of God, even bring God to others in a mysterious way. Frederick Buechner reflects on this, stating,

> I have it in me at my best to be a saint to other people, and by saint I mean life-giver, someone who is able to bear to others something of the Holy Spirit, whom the creeds describe as the Lord and Giver of Life. Sometimes, by the grace of God, I have it in me to be Christ to other people. And so, of course, have we all—the life-giving, life-saving, and healing power to be saints . . . maybe at rare moments even to ourselves. I believe that it is when that power is alive in me and through me that I come closest to being truly home.[21]

To chat about over tea, coffee, and/or chocolate:

Describe your community and the relationships you have with those who form it. Is there something you would change about your community if you could? And if you have no community, what actions can you take to belong to a community?

Do you "work on yourself" and do you bring your authentic self to others? Why or why not? How do you bring yourself to others?

Which of the habits of Jesus' relationships with others are easiest for you? Which are most challenging? (Jesus' habits include befriending the powerless, loving his enemies, being both compassionate and challenging, and walking with others in pain and joy.)

---

21. Buechner, *The Longing for Home*; quoted in Meyers, *The Allure of Hope*, 171.

Do you tend toward being overly independent or overly dependent? How can you move toward interdependence?

What goals are you pursuing with regard to your relationships with others?

Prayer

O, Trinitarian God who is forever in community, grant that I may be so transformed into your image that I may fellowship in community as you are in community. Show me myself to that I can bring her to others; empower me to be like Jesus in relationships, and guide me into interdependence. As Jesus heals, please heal relational areas in my life that need it; as the Holy Spirit leads, please lead me into relationships that are glorifying to you in all ways. May I be so transformed that I am able to bless and bring wholeness to the people of this broken world. I pray this in the name of the Son, to the glory of the Father, and by the power of the Holy Spirit.

Amen.

10

Girlfriends

Relating to Other Women

The more a daughter knows the details of her mother's life . . .
the stronger the daughter.

~ ANITA DIAMANT, *THE RED TENT*

Some women pray for their daughters to marry good husbands. I pray that my
girls will find girlfriends half as loyal and true as the Ya-Yas.

~ REBECCA WELLS, *DIVINE SECRETS*
OF THE YA-YA SISTERHOOD

God did not create you to be alone. He deposited skills, knowledge, and talents
in someone out there who is expected to mentor you, teach you and encourage
you to go high. Go, get a mentor!

~ ISRAELMORE AYIVOR, GHANAIAN CHRISTIAN,
MOTIVATIONAL SPEAKER, AND AUTHOR

SINCE MY YOUTH, I'VE been one to find myself more at ease in the company
of other women than in the company of men, even though I was a tomboy.
Perhaps it was my closeness with my mother and her model of great friendships with other women, or my consistent failure in physical competitions

with my older brother (I like to win). I don't know why, but friendships with women were always easier.

For some who participate in *Woman*, relationships with other women is commonplace, while others prefer relationships with men. Possibly the main function of the rite of passage is to create space to talk about being a Christian woman with peers and with women who are further along in the journey. Both relationships with women and with men are vital to our lives, interdependence, and healthy community. It is good to relate with those who are similar as well as with those who are different.

Sometimes our difficulty relating with other women as peers stems from the fact that we are uncomfortable with being a woman. At other times, it stems from a preference to avoid topics of conversation or stereotypical actions that are often apparent among groups of women. At still other times, it stems from our failure to embrace our own stories. Rather than focus on what we have, we sometimes focus on what we lack and compare ourselves to others.

> Comparison can take many forms. We may compare our weight, skin complexion, hair, clothes, families, whether or not we are dating, who we are dating, how successful we are in school, our spirituality, what kind of car we drive—the list is endless. A friend once told me that when she walks into a room, she immediately critiques what everyone is wearing and then ranks where she fits relative to the woman wearing the best outfit. Her ranking determines whether or not she's having a good day.[1]

Some of us are always trying to come out ahead; others have chosen to deliberately come out behind in order not to face unchosen failure. Comparison is destructive to our interpersonal relationships.

It is far better to know and understand yourself and bring your best self to the relationships, realizing that your expression and your voice are different from others', and neither better nor worse. Rather than being in competition, we can seek interdependence. Participants in *Woman* and you who are doing this book with a group have the unique opportunity to interact with women who are different from you, but who share a common journey right now. What a privilege! If one of the others intimidates you, be sure to have coffee or a meal with her so that you can understand your peer relationship and find your commonalities. The journey of womanhood is

---

1. Dean, "Friends or Enemies?," 121.

not a race and it is not measured. Do your best to keep moving forward together.

Friends as Family

Once, years ago, a college student came to me desirous to be freed from several oppressive habits and to move forward in a healthy manner in her life. I had her write out her goals and invited her to my home, where we would pray together, assisting in her healing and progress. I was surprised at the diverse group of friends that she invited to my house to be with her in this process. Numbering about five, I asked them how they knew each other, and as they affectionately told their stories, they always referred to each other as family. Some came from broken homes and others from intact ones, but together they had formed family bonds that they hoped would last.

Camerin Courtney wrote *Table for One: The Savvy Girl's Guide to Singleness,* in which she reveals much about her life as a single woman. She has a close group of four female friends and also calls them family, writing, "I don't use the word 'family' lightly here. The relationships I share with these dear Christian sisters goes deep and represent a serious investment of time."[2] She has not come to embrace this family because of brokenness in her home of origin, but rather has embraced it because it has been offered to her. She believes that making close friends takes patience, prayer, and risks, as well as always being open to having more people in the group.[3]

Liminal *Communitas*

Many people look back on their college years as a time when they made close friends that last for a lifetime. The college environment is special and unique, all working toward graduation, but all doing so in varied ways. College can be a rite of passage in itself—if you move away to attend school, that is the rite of separation; the four years of study is the liminal rite of transition, and graduation is reincorporation with new privileges and responsibilities. The liminal stage for *Woman* participants is the time period between Initiation and the Crossing Over Ceremony, when they read this

2. Courtney, *Table for One*, 78.

3. Ibid., 86–87.

book with others. And whether you've gone to college or not, you can likely think of transitional times in your life, sometimes alone and sometimes in the company of others.

In this liminal transition, ritual theorist Victor Turner has seen that a special camaraderie is formed and he calls it *communitas*.[4] While other stages in life are hierarchical, this is a company of equals where people bond in a very deep manner. When you look around you at a *Woman* meeting, when you get together with those who read this book with you, you will always remember that you went through this process with them. Why not seek to form long-standing bonds with others in this journey that will continue for life?

Sibling in Christ

When I teach Christian thought, we discuss the *ordo salutis,* a list of all the "steps" or all parts of the process of becoming a Christian. Though it is a bit "boxy" and makes something organic into a series of specific steps, it is also useful because it makes us realize the depth of all the blessings of salvation. One of the steps is adoption.

Though we've talked about having friends as family, we take this one step further as Christians. We have been adopted to be part of the family of God. And with God as our Father, all other Christians are our brothers and sisters. Often, we concentrate on our relationship to God as Father, paying less attention to our relationships as siblings.

When I teach adoption, I like to tell a story of my childhood. I was a middle child, with an older brother and younger sister. My brother didn't always get along with the other boys in the neighborhood, and one day one of those boys approached me as I walked down the street to my friend's house. He came close and punched me hard in my shoulder, saying, "That's for your brother." As he was two years older than I, I was terrified and completed the walk to my friend's house in tears. After a phone call with my mother calmed me down, I spent the rest of the afternoon playing. But, if you are a brother or know any good brothers, you know what happened later that evening. My brother made an appointment with that boy to meet at a place where they sometimes engaged in fistfights. The last hard punch to the stomach that my brother gave him was accompanied by the words, "That's for my sister." No one messes with our brother or sister in our real

4. Turner, *The Ritual Process*, 127.

families. That's the relationship we are privileged to have with those in the family of Christ—we are siblings in Christ.

At the risk of sounding like a sorority,[5] I encourage you to love your sisters, uphold your sisters, and deeply share this journey of womanhood. You will find personal growth and great blessing as you do.

Relationships with Older Women

Not only does *Woman* encourage relationships with one another, but also with women who are further along in the journey. Though relationships with younger women are also important, this journey concentrates on forward progress, so the focus is on relationships with older women.

I recall a time in my life when I lived in a small town in Pennsylvania. I was a "transplant" there, coming from my teaching time in Paraguay where I had many female peer relationships. I use the term *transplant* because the stereotypical native grew up there, attended the local Penn State branch campus and then the main campus, and returned to marry their high school sweetheart. It felt like a rather closed community. There, all the women in church were married and many were having children, so I had no single peers. Having come from a close-knit community in Paraguay, I felt deep loss.

And though that was a lonely time, I found friendships in the most surprising places. Some of my closest female friends were over sixty. And I met regularly with a mom that I respected who was at least ten years my senior. Peer relationships are great, but relationships with older women have greatness in them, too.

The people you choose to have in your community change you. When I wrote my first article about *Woman*, I was surprised as I measured the growth shown by the differences between the intake survey and the exit survey.[6] That year, the process was only one semester with four meetings total. Though we did not discuss areas like leadership or the equality of male and female in our direct teaching, the participants rated themselves significantly higher in those areas at the end than they had at the beginning. One even wrote, "One of the things that I gained was that power and

---

5. I only state it's risky because some sororities do not have great reputations; however, I think the concept of a sisterhood and the fierce loyalty shown to one another in sororities is impressive!

6. Davis Abdallah, "Development and Efficacy of a Rite of Passage."

authority . . . come with knowing Scripture and understanding it. This was gained through the witness of [one of the leaders]. The way they were able to use and understand the Word and how it relates to and impacts their life was so powerful." The participants "caught" more than we "taught" them. If you develop relationships with mature older women, you will likely "catch" much from them!

Mothers and Mentors

I have been blessed to always have a close relationship with my mother. Anne Frank wrote, "Mummy herself has told us that she looked upon us more as her friends than her daughters. Now that is all very fine, but still, a friend can't take a mother's place."[7] Some of us have friendships with our mothers, some do not know our mothers, some have both biological and adoptive mothers, some relationships are strained, and others are broken. Each story is different.

In fact, the way we relate to our mothers and others is often different according to the culture from which we come. The brevity of this book does not allow me to put it all in cultural perspective, but culture forms the way we understand many relationships, especially family ones. Kathy Khang writes about how being a girl was viewed in her Asian culture: "For some of us the deepest pain is being a daughter and failing to meet the cultural expectation to be a son. Cultures once deeply agrarian needed, literally, manpower. Women were not always valued or celebrated—they were simply necessary for their role in producing the family heirs."[8] Khang also points out that her parents had different expectations for her than her non-Asian friends. Not only was she expected to excel academically and have nice Korean Christian friends in college, but she was also to spend weekends at home helping with her parents' business and attending church with them.[9] Different families have differing expectations and relationships with their daughters; some of those differences fall along cultural lines.

Some of us, both those with good mother-daughter relationships, and those with poor ones, have found spiritual mothers in mentors. I must confess that I've never had a formal mentor, though I've had many

7. Anne Frank, *Diary of a Young Girl,* as quoted in McMinn, *Growing Strong Daughters,* 185.

8. Khang, "Pulled by Expectations," 37.

9. Ibid., 39.

older women influence my life. Seeking formal and informal mentoring facilitates our growth. Mentors can help us in many areas, as the following quotes from *Woman* participants emphasize:

"My mentoring relationship helped me to receive a different perspective on things in my life. Through my mentoring relationship I have gained a close friend."

"I gained a picture of and insight into the life of a woman honestly seeking to follow God in her context. She is a wife and mother, a missionary, a Sunday school teacher, and I learned from watching her life with God in all of her roles. I was able to see what it looks like for her to love, and nurture, for her to trust God in hard times etc. We cooked together, we talked about nature, we talked about the word of God."

"I have learned more about handling my ethnic identity through the experiences of my mentor."

"It was encouraging to talk with a woman who has been through similar struggles."

"My mentoring relationship has been fantastic. It has truly taught me how to connect with other women and be real with them. While some of her advice and guidance has been hard, like being alone for a certain amount of time every week, I have found it necessary. This has been the first formal mentoring relationship I have ever had and it is something that I want to continue."

"It has been good to discuss things with my mentor and get a different perspective from what I would get from friends my own age or from an older family member."

"She really helped me understand what it is to be me and to be a woman outside of a relationship with a man. She also helped me understand how I have grown."

Many people, when assigned to a new occupation, receive a mentor, since mentoring is done quite frequently in all areas of life today. *Woman* participants as well as other readers might look for more of a spiritual mentor who can guide them in the journey of Christian womanhood. It is important to choose a woman that you respect, whose life journey has some important similarities to yours as well as some differences, someone with whom you will be able to be completely open, someone who will challenge you and have compassion on you, and someone who has qualities that you wish to emulate.

If no one you know fits the criteria, try someone you do not know very well, but do not choose too quickly. Be willing to spend at least an hour with the possible mentor, finding out whether it will be a good "fit." Before meeting her, think through the areas where you would like to grow and find out if she would be able to help you in those areas. If one does not "fit," try another, and do not be discouraged! We don't find the "mentor spark" with everyone.

I find that successful mentoring relationships come from mentees who fully "buy in" to the process. When a mentee does the following, she will increase both the success of the relationship and her personal growth.

- Pursue the relationship. If the mentor cancels, be sure to follow up and reschedule; when you need the mentor's help, ask; be on time to meetings and do your best to assure regular meetings. If she has agreed to mentor you, be gracious when she has other obligations, but do not back off for fear of being a burden, unless she tells you to.

- Be open and honest. If you hide from your mentor, you will lessen your own growth.

- Listen and follow through. Though your mentor may not always be right, be willing to listen to and trust her. Even if you want to rebel against some of her advice as she challenges you, trust that she has your good in mind and try what she suggests. If she gives you an assignment, complete it quickly and efficiently, not at the last minute.

- Ask for what you need. Do not wait until the end of the meeting to bring up the issue you really want to talk about, but bring it up at the beginning and ask for help.

Always keep in mind, however, that a mentor is not your Savior. Only Jesus is, and your mentor will frequently point you to Jesus. Whether your first key mentor is your mother or another person who becomes a spiritual or adoptive mother, do your best to nurture the success of the relationship, and allow it to grow and change you.

Women to Interview

An important assignment in *Woman* is that of interviewing older women that the participants respect about the journey of womanhood, and I encourage other readers to do the interviews as well. Many younger women have never asked an older woman about what it means to be a woman, when she felt like when she became a woman, or how she experienced any other aspects of life as a woman. Though the participants are bit timid as they first think about the interviews, they are universally pleased with the outcome, and many want to keep interviewing women since the exercise is so helpful. If it is difficult to think of questions to ask, some suggested questions include:

- When did you begin to "own" the title "woman"?
- What is (are) the rite(s) of passage that you experienced on your journey toward womanhood?
- How would you describe your confidence?
- How do you understand sexuality and physical well-being?
- What are three things you wished you knew about womanhood and life when you were my age?
- What are your proudest moments as a woman and the moments you are most ashamed of?
- How do you define womanhood?
- What do you love about being a woman?
- What words of advice do you have for me on your journey?
- If she's single, ask her about it; if she's married, ask her about it.

An interview is a good way to deepen a relationship by learning the other's story. It is a good way to interact on a more profound level with moms and grandmas, aunts or cousins, for they have often formed our understanding of womanhood and we are part of the line of women in our family. Connecting to the women in our family can be enriching and surprising, often in a good way. If one finds, however, that the line of women in her family has many she wishes *not* to emulate, interviewing and creating relationships with other women reminds her of her heritage in the family of God. The helpfulness of the interviews is explained in the women's own words:

"The interviews with other women helped me to realize that a lot of women have the same struggles I did or do."

"I gained so much great advice and perspective from older women and I *love* talking to older women. Talking to them is like reading an encyclopedia on life as a woman. My advice for the women coming in is to talk to women who are in different walks of life and different ages in life. My interviewees ranged from their thirties to their seventies."

"I gained different perspectives from married and unmarried women. I also interviewed two missionaries, one single and one married. It was interesting to get their perspective on womanhood in other cultures. The recommendation that I have for others is to interview different people, so that you get different answers to the same questions."

"I was discouraged at one interview because she seemed to underestimate her authority as a woman. Being someone that I looked up to for a long time, this was surprising. The rest were inspiration and showed me how to live confidently as a woman."

"The interviews went well. I learned a lot about my heritage and found ways that I want to change my relationships now to break patterns. I would recommend people interview not only women they admire but a few women they don't, to understand both positive traits they would like to possess and negative traits they would like to avoid."

"Most women are willing to share their life and life experiences with younger women, and we should certainly take advantage."

"The interviews were amazing. Through it I gained a deeper relationship with my sister-in-law, a better way to understand my worth and embrace my body, and a deepened understanding of the importance of sexuality and maintaining purity."

Although the process of *Woman* invites participants to have formal interviews with older women, it was simply a specific way to gain wisdom and vicarious experience from others. A less formal way to gain that wisdom is to tell our own stories to others as well as to listen to one another's stories. There is much to be gained from older women, whether moms, mentors, or simply those who have gone before. You can also gain lifelong friendships with women your own age, right now. Don't let the opportunity pass you by!

I cannot conclude this chapter on relationships with other women without acknowledging same-sex attraction and same-sex relationships. Unfortunately, the scope of this work does not leave me room to fully explore this area in a fair manner. We know that the church is split on this; some denominations accept same-sex marriage while others find homosexuality sinful. For those who have questions about this area, I recommend finding books solely dedicated to it. I recommend Wesley Hill and Kristyn Komarnicki's books, articles, and blogs on the topic.

To chat about over tea, coffee, and/or chocolate:

Do you prefer relationships with men or women? Why do you avoid one and concentrate on the other? How can you be more balanced?

Do you have friends you consider family? Who are they and how did they arrive to that place?

What is your relationship with your mother like? How has it formed you?

How is your relationship with your mentor? How did you choose her?

What goals are you pursuing with regard to your relationships with others?

Prayer

O, Trinitarian God who is forever in community, grant that I may be so transformed into your image that I may fellowship in community as you are in community. Show me myself so that I can bring her to others; empower me to be like Jesus in relationships, and guide me into interdependence. As Jesus heals, please heal relational areas in my life that need it; as the Holy Spirit leads, please lead me into relationships that are glorifying to you in all ways; and as Father parents, please bring me mentors, spiritual mothers and fathers that will nurture and challenge me. May I be so transformed that I am able to bless and bring wholeness to the people of this broken world. I pray this in the name of the Son, to the glory of the Father, and by the power of the Holy Spirit.

Amen.

11

Harry Was Wrong

Women and Men as Friends and Colleagues

"A woman needs a man like a fish needs a bicycle." I really hate this expression.
I bet fish would totally want bicycles.

~ MEG CABOT, *PRINCESS ON THE BRINK*

There's different kinds of love, and I'd never experienced that kind of totally
platonic love. All the love I've experienced has always been a kind of deal, and
now, as I get older, I realize that there's this other love out there.

~ TRACY EMIN, CYPRIOT ENGLISH ARTIST

People instantly assume you can't have a platonic friendship with someone of
the opposite sex. I think this may be specific to L. A.—or America.

~ ISABEL LUCAS, AUSTRALIAN ACTRESS

Men are from Earth, women are from Earth. Deal with it.

~ GEORGE CARLIN, AMERICAN COMEDIAN AND WRITER

AFTER MY SOPHOMORE YEAR of college, I spent the summer working at a
school and living with my grandfather on Long Island. I had often heard

that the movie *When Harry Met Sally* was amusing, so one evening, we rented it. *Bad idea*. Imagine sitting through significant sexual commentary with your grandfather sitting beside you . . . or don't imagine it—it's too embarrassing.

When Harry Met Sally is famous for popularizing the idea that men and women can't be friends. In a conversation the two have in a restaurant, Harry seeks to convince Sally that men and women can't be friends because the desire for sexual intercourse gets in the way. According to him, though Sally thought she had platonic male friendships, she didn't, because men want sex with any female. She concludes that she and Harry can't be friends with a sigh, since he's the only person she knows in the city.[1]

Harry's notion that male-female friendship is impossible was nothing new, and I grew up in a culture that completely agreed with it. However, like many today, I question Harry's blanket statement and rue the lack of self-control it assumes of mankind. In fact, though I agree that not *all* men can be friends with *all* women, female-male friendships are healthy, needed, and instrumental for portraying the full image of God to the world.

For some women on the journey of womanhood, relationships with men are not preferred, perhaps because of a lack of relationship with their fathers, fear of the opposite sex due to negative stereotypes or experiences, lack of experience, or various other reasons. On the other hand, some would want to read this chapter first because it is top priority for them!

I recently visited a monastery, and am fascinated by those who choose a solitary life. Though monks and nuns still have relationships with the opposite sex, they are not fraught with questions of genital sexuality, but are instead person-to-person relationships without that pressure. Not that monks or nuns are perfect or immune to falling in love—Jesuit James Martin is honest enough to tell that he had fallen in love, but had chosen his vocation over that love (not that it was simple, but it was a choice).[2] Nuns' and monks' devotion to God and celibacy lends them a kind of freedom that others do not have.

I have met many women who I think would be very happy as nuns—studying, serving, and working with their hands. I've also met others who act like they are called to permanent celibacy because they do not pursue healthy male friendships; they think God will just drop "Mr. Right" into

1. Ephron, *When Harry Met Sally*.
2. Martin, *My Life with the Saints,* 204–5, 231.

their laps and they will not only immediately recognize him, but also be ready for him. Some act more like Disney princesses than true humans.

Permanent celibacy is a choice, as being truly open to (not avoiding) relationships with men is also a choice. Either choice is fine—a life with nonsexualized relationships, or one with the potential of marriage and children. A life of female-only friends, however, does not prepare one well for either life. Also, men tend to be able to sense whether a woman is truly open to having a relationship with them—all humans sense whether another person is truly open. Regardless of whether one chooses marriage, choosing to have relationships with men (the non-dating kind) is healthy. Men and women need each other—singly, we cannot express the image of God, but together as family, we begin to approximate its diversity, wealth, and beauty.

'Ezer Kenegdo

To comprehend female-male relationships, we need to once again return to the creation account in Genesis. We've learned about the image of God there, the fact that we need community, and now we investigate why and how Eve was created, as described in Genesis 2.

Adam has been formed from the dust, and proceeds to name all the animals, a process that simply accentuates his loneliness, showing his need for a helper like him.[3] The term used to describe her in Genesis 2:18 is 'ezer kenegdo in Hebrew, variously translated "helper suitable for him" (NIV and NASB), "helper as his partner" (NRSV), and "helper fit for him" (ESV). "Helper" is designated in each translation, and yet it is not referring to subordination, as in "mommy's little helper." 'Ezer in Scripture is usually used to refer to God as the "'helper' for Israel or for an individual who appeals to him."[4] Of the twenty-one times this term is used in Scripture, fourteen refer to God and four to military rescue.[5] If God is helper, this word for helper does not refer to God being subordinate and must thus not necessarily refer to woman's subordination.

---

3. Hess, "Equality with and without Innocence," 84.
4. Ibid., 86.
5. Haddad, "Why Did God Create Woman?"

R. David Freedman further defines *'ezer* as proceeding from "two He-brew roots that mean 'to rescue, to save' and 'to be strong.'"[6] Author and leader Mimi Haddad explains,

> The quality of Eve's help is never that of an inferior or subordinate. Eve by definition was created to lend a vital form of power. When you remember "woman's creational DNA" as *ezer* [sic]—as strong help, it explains two perplexing issues. First, it shows how women, as a whole, never perform according to the cultural devaluation made of them. Throughout history and within Scripture, we ob-serve women's successful leadership, which, I tell my students, is a fact not readily incorporated into Christian curricula used in churches, colleges or seminaries. Second, if *ezer* is woman's "cre-ational DNA," this also explains why women are so devastated and demoralized when churches fail to recognize their God-intended purposes. Treating females as inferior and subordinate violates an essential component of their calling as *ezer*. And it also explains why the more we recognize women as powerful help, the more they in turn extend strong help to others.[7]

Eve was not a "frail beauty to rescue" or a "weak, waif-like, dependent creature,"[8] but rather a strong help who helps like God does.

Furthermore, she was created from Adam's rib, which "actually refers to the side of the man, a part of the body that is neither above or below him."[9] Old Testament professor Richard Hess concludes, "The woman was formed from the man as his 'corresponding helper' or partner, with no im-plication of inferiority or subordination."[10] In fact, the first words out of Adam's mouth to describe her are "bone of my bones" showing his recogni-tion of their similarity and partnership.

I believe that women are corresponding partners not only to the men whom they marry, but also to other women and men with whom they form friendships or partner with in various endeavors. To enact this "creational DNA" is a high calling indeed.

---

6. As cited in Haddad, "Why Did God Create Woman?"
7. Ibid.
8. Haddad, "Are Women Fully Human?"
9. Hess, "Equality with and without Innocence," 86.
10. Ibid., 94.

Sexuality

For my Masters of Divinity internship, I worked in a church and my mentor was a male pastor. Though I was twenty-seven and he was seventy-two, he refused to ever meet with me alone, wanting to assure that there was no possibility for sexual temptation between us. While he meant well, it was sometimes difficult to find public places to meet when we could not drive together; working together was complicated, and even had we met individually, I don't think our relationship would have become sexualized.

In their book, *Singled Out: Why Celibacy Must be Reinvented in Today's Church*, Christine Colón and Bonnie Field tell a similar story of their friend, a single, modest, kind Christian woman who worked for a Christian company. "She was under the impression that being single would be an advantage in the workplace because she could leave on a business trip at a moment's notice. But she was told quite plainly that the opposite was true. Because she was a single woman, the men of the company had to bring their wives along on a business trip as chaperones. If their wives did not come [she would have to stay in a separate *hotel* and go to dinner *alone*]."[11] The underlying belief of the company was that people cannot resist sexual temptation, so the only way to deal with it is to avoid it altogether through chaperones and separation.

Colón and Field see this as one of several dangerous messages given to the people of the church.[12] In stating that we cannot resist sexual temptation, the church is actually agreeing with the world, rather than understanding humanity in a redeemed sense. The idea that sexual temptation always happens in male-female relationships is from cultural works like *When Harry Met Sally*, not from the Bible. Men and women can work together without having sexual intercourse. There may not even be sexual temptation between them, but if there is, it *can be resisted*.

The dangerous and false message that sexual temptation cannot be resisted also affects dating couples. It has often resulted in unmarried people doing every sexual act possible outside of intercourse, and only focusing on outward behaviors.[13] Many interpret sexual acts as only outward and physical with no spiritual or soul-ish factors or effects. They then assume that if they avoid the stimulus (being alone with someone of the opposite sex)

11. Colón and Field, *Singled Out*, 104; emphasis added.
12. Ibid., 100.
13. Ibid., 101.

then they can avoid the physical sin. On the contrary, sexuality has more to do with our souls than our bodies—it is our *interpretation* of stimuli that needs redemption, not the stimuli themselves.[14] That is, looking at the opposite sex as an object of sexual desire more than as a fellow human is the problem; the problem is not the fact that he or she is attractive.

I remember walking in the *souq* (bazaar) in Damascus, Syria. We walked down a wide middle aisle, and all the shopkeepers were on either side. A Muslim woman walked in front of us. She wore the traditional flowing all-black garment and only her face was uncovered. I was shocked as I saw one of the shopkeepers stare lustfully at her as she came toward him, passed, and went on. He practically licked his lips at her shapeless form and could not take his eyes off her. Here, it was clear that the stimulus was not the problem. She was not being seductive in any apparent way. Rather, the problem was his interpretation. It seemed that regardless of her dress or relationship to him, he understood that women were to be lusted after. And he had no need to control himself—after all, aren't all women temptresses?

Unfortunately, beliefs such as this pervade even the church. I gave a presentation to a group of male and female students in which I stated that it is insulting to men to think that they cannot avoid sexual temptation when confronted by attractive women. I think men have the power of self-control. One of the male students told me afterward that he felt freed by that statement. It was getting close to spring, and at this time of the year, he had been taught to think, "Oh no! I will soon see women with less clothing on! How will I avoid the sexual temptation?" The presentation reminded him that he used to look forward to spring and had never really been deeply affected by the clothing issue; he could release himself from fear of "spring lust." As he changed his interpretation of the stimuli, he found freedom.

Indeed, unlike him, some men have reason to be concerned when spring rolls around because they have a history of either giving in to sexual temptation or difficulty in resisting at this time; everyone is different. However, St. Anthony of the desert, a fourth-century monk in Egypt who lived a solitary life, was still sexually tempted even without external stimuli. We cannot simply avoid all sexual temptation. It is a matter of the interpretation, a matter of the soul, rather than the stimuli.

Please note that it is certainly good to avoid or flee sexual temptation, but to think that sexual temptation is part and parcel to any meeting of the sexes is simply not true. John Stott, Christian leader, writer, and lifelong

14. Ibid., 105.

celibate believes we can resist sexual temptation. "We Christians must insist that self-control is possible. We have learned to control our temper, our tongue, our greed, our jealousy, our pride: why should it be thought impossible to control our libido? To say that we cannot is to deny our dignity as human beings and to descend to the level of animals, which are creatures of uncontrolled instinct."[15] We are called to self-control; after all, it is part of the blessing of the fruit of the Spirit (Gal 5:22–23). In spite of examples to the contrary, many have been faithful, celibate Christians.

Lust can be avoided. In my Christian thought class, we have been known to chat about whether Jesus ever had an erection. Though some may think this query sacrilegious, the fact that we believe Jesus was fully human begs the question. I think it's possible that Jesus had an erection—it seems that it happens with varying frequency to men, and not always in response to stimuli. This, however, does not mean that Jesus necessarily lusted. Wesley Hill has a helpful definition of lust in his book, *Washed and Waiting*. He states that we may look around and see someone to whom we are attracted—that's not lust. The look becomes lust when it lingers and turns our thoughts. Looking and lingering and imagining is lust.[16] We cannot avoid ever seeing attractive people. Jesus, being fully human, may have seen someone he thought was attractive and may have had an involuntary physical response. However, because he resisted temptation in his Spirit-anointed humanity, that look did not linger and turn into lust. Sexual purity does not mean never having a thought about sex or never noticing someone attractive. Remember—it's not about the stimuli, but about the response to it. Sexual purity means yielding to the Holy Spirit and not turning to lust. It also means exercising self-control by maintaining appropriate physical sexual boundaries and working on our interpretations of stimuli. It *is* possible.

Since sexual temptation can be avoided, does this mean that we should throw ourselves into any and all relationships with men? Certainly not. Relationships require discernment. While cross-gender friendships can be safe, not all are, so some caution and discernment is necessary. Barton states that cross-gender relationships have degrees of safety. "In a friendship where both parties take full responsibility for themselves by being self-aware, dealing with their own issues and being honest, loving, and

15. As quoted in Colón and Field, *Singled Out*, 105.

16. Hill, *Washed and Waiting*, 135–37. Hill cites Dallas Willard, *The Divine Conspiracy*, for this definition.

disciplined in their behavior, the degree of safety can be increased dramatically. On the other hand, when one or both parties renege on their personal responsibility by living an unexamined life, being undisciplined or placing blame on others, the relationship involves much more risk."[17]

In addition, there may be times when sexual attraction happens within a cross-gender relationship that should not be acted on. For parties that cannot manage their sexuality, they may need to then avoid the relationship. For those that can, Barton recommends stating openly that the chemistry is there, and thus robbing it of its mystique. She also recommends stating a commitment to each other that they will not "cross the line" by instigating "physical contact that is sexually motivated."[18]

Our sexuality is part of who we are, and while it is our desire for connectedness, it can sometimes also be a desire for sexual intercourse. Those desires *can* be resisted, and it is actually possible to have good relationships with men, married and single, that do not end up in the bedroom. I can remember avoiding many relationships for fear that "he might be interested in me." May we no longer lose the beauty of cross-gender friendships for such a reason! McMinn has helpful ideas that formed her plan for her daughters to have healthy relationships with men. "We defined healthy in the following four ways. First, that our daughters were honest and direct in their communication rather than coy and indirect. Second, that they were confident in their ability to be equal partners in the friendship. Third, that they were able to appreciate differences that make relationships with the other gender interesting and fulfilling. And fourth, that they would be interdependent not only in their relationships but also in seeking input regarding those relationships."[19]

Commonalities and Partnering

John Gray's *Men Are From Mars, Women Are From Venus* has sold millions of copies and has given many the ability to understand the differences between men and women, for we sometimes puzzle one another. Focusing only on differences and never on similarities, however, may miss the bigger picture since we are both *actually* from planet earth, originally formed from dust and one another. Though we use the term "opposite sex," we are

17. Barton, *Equal to the Task,* 201.

18. Ibid., 205.

19. McMinn, *Growing Strong Daughters,* 63.

more like each other than anything else around.[20] The male and female stereotypes that many believe are exaggerated forms of the truth obscure what we share in common,[21] and allow for little diversity among people—many individuals break stereotypical molds for their gender. So, while at times it is helpful to understand differences, it is perhaps even more important to focus on commonalities between women and men.

When Adam exclaimed, "bone of my bones and flesh of my flesh," he was praising the similarities, not the differences. Mimi Haddad insightfully points out, "Scripture does not emphasize the differences between Adam and Eve, as many do today. Rather, Scripture points to the *unity* and oneness of Adam and Eve. They share a physical body, because Eve comes from Adam's body. And, most significantly, they also share the same spiritual or metaphysical substance because they are both created in God's image."[22] Let us follow the biblical example to remember and focus on what we have in common in order to strengthen partnerships between men and women!

Genesis 3 narrates the fall of humankind, and most interpretations see more than just fruit-eating as the cause. Barton sees the fall as a failure on the part of the humans to act as a team; the first human couple failed to give and receive feedback and to make decisions together.[23] Eve did not consult Adam (who was with her [Gen 3:6]), but spoke only to the serpent and made the decision to partake of the fruit. Adam did not talk with Eve about the advisability of the serpent's plan but decided to eat the fruit she gave to him. Choosing not to truly partner meant they distorted their image-bearing call to steward the earth together.

> Ultimately, the struggle that women and men experience as they try to live, work and minister together is spiritual in nature; it is one result of the terrible tearing that occurred in the community of two that God created in the beginning. God was not the only one who realized how effective true teamwork can be; Satan must have also understood how effective the male-female partnership would be in accomplishing God's purposes, for he wasted no time in attempting to undermine it.[24]

---

20. Elaine Storkey, as cited in Barton, *Equal to the Task,* 80.

21. Barton, *Equal to the Task,* 84.

22. Haddad, "Identity and Creation in Christ (Part I)."

23. Barton, *Equal to the Task,* 29.

24. Ibid., 28.

Ever since, partnership between male and female has been full of struggle and often tenuous due to various personal, professional, and relational issues.

Fear is the main reason that women do not partner with men, according to Barton. The fact that many women have not opened ourselves to learn and experience men as partners makes us unprepared for feelings that may surface during our close partnership with them.[25] While we should be cautious in a society full of affairs, divorce, and casual sex, the time has come to look beyond our societal issues and ask, "Are relationships ruled by fear and mistrust all we can hope for in the family of God? Our fears and failures point to our great need for biblically functioning community [where] 'genderedness,' rather than being used to limit and exploit others, is honored, respected, and even celebrated as the great gift that it is."[26] In partnering relationships, we must acknowledge our fears, our limitations, and our sexuality, while at the same time intentionally moving forward into relationships of wholeness as whole persons.

Partnership *is* possible between men and women in the church and in society. It comes when we cultivate our own and others' gifts on a team, rather than competing and allowing our differing gifts to be diminished.[27] Though this only comes through practice and may include setbacks along the way, it is important to allow our voices to be heard in all their distinctiveness and diversity. Even in war and police work, areas traditionally dominated by men, women's voices should be heard at the table, partnering with men. Women's intuitiveness has proven them better than men at calming violent situations since they can more easily read the ambiguous situations that police confront.[28] "If women are predisposed to be better communicators, are better able to read nonverbal cues, are capable of making intuitive judgments of character and events, and are more committed to peaceful alternatives than men, then they may be better suited for positions dealing with foreign affairs and national security."[29]

McMinn tells the story of a male physicist who was determining the number of immediate fatalities that would result from various counterattacks in a war. One particular strategy would result in thirty million deaths

25. Ibid., 50.

26. Ibid., 51.

27. Ibid., 119.

28. McMinn, *Growing Strong Daughters*, 44.

29. Ibid.

rather than thirty-six million, and all were impressed at the decrease. The physicist suddenly realized how ridiculous it was to state *only* thirty million immediate fatalities, and blurted out his dismay. No one responded, and he felt like a woman because he was thinking about *people* rather than *strategy.*[30]

Furthermore, a Vietnam veteran was appalled by his peers' destruction of shrines, sexuality, and livelihoods during his tour; he felt this behavior counteracted any gain on the battlefield. For this reason, he believed if a woman were in charge of the troops, a different perspective and influence would balance peacekeeping efforts.[31]

By no means am I seeking to state that previously male-dominated fields should become female-dominated fields. Rather, I suggest partnering in *all* fields. Both male and female voices bring distinct and necessary perspectives to situations; the presence of *both* brings balance. Males in traditionally female-dominated fields (education, nursing, etc.) would also offer better balance and partnering to the world. We have been created to partner, and though it may be difficult to be a pioneer in these areas, it will be worth it; partnership brings about better life for the world, for we share a common humanity.

Harry *was* wrong. And though his assertion has pervaded society, we can seek opportunities to enter conversations and partnerships with other men and women as the fiery work of the Holy Spirit restores our "creational DNA," the image of the triune God.

To chat about over tea, coffee, and/or chocolate:

Describe your relationships with men—older, younger, peer. How do you think you can improve them?

How do you understand *'ezer kenegdo*? How will that affect how you relate to men?

Do you agree with the idea that sexual temptation can be avoided in friendships and partnerships with men? Why or why not?

What goals are you pursuing with regard to your relationships with others?

30. Ibid.
31. Ibid., 45.

Prayer

O, Trinitarian God who is forever in community, grant that I may be so transformed into your image that I may fellowship in community as you are in community. Show me myself so that I can bring her to others; empower me to be like Jesus in relationships, and guide me into interdependence. Empower me to resist sexual temptation and guide me into friendships and partnerships with men. As Jesus heals, please heal relational areas in my life that need it; as the Holy Spirit leads, please lead me into relationships that are glorifying to you in all ways; and as the Father parents, please bring me mentors, spiritual mothers and fathers, that will nurture and challenge me. May I be so transformed that I am able to bless and bring wholeness to the people of this broken world. I pray this in the name of the Son, to the glory of the Father, and by the power of the Holy Spirit.

Amen.

12

Doing Life Solo

Enjoying Singleness

I'm OK with being single, but I'm not OK when the time comes where I have to move my furniture around and to change the high ceiling light balls.

~ HIROKO SAKAI, JAPANESE ARTIST

When asked why I am single, my reply is simply; I consider myself a black pearl rare in my authenticity, adding a mysterious beauty to the select few who can recognize & even fewer who appreciate my worth. So instead of dating, I throw myself into working in the field. If my Boaz recognizes me amongst the black rocks . . . great! If not, the magnificence of my rarity will simply radiate onto those working the fields as well in the form of teaching, which is what I do.

~ SANJO JENDAYI, EMPOWERMENT SPEAKER,
AUTHOR, AND SPOKEN WORD ARTIST

You don't have to be part of a couple to be happy, you know.

~ PHYLLIS REYNOLDS NAYLOR, WRITER

THOUGH WE MAY HAVE opportunities to partner in the church and society, not all of us have opportunities for a male life partner. The majority of people marry at some point in their lives, but not everyone does, and the median age for a first marriage is steadily increasing (about 27 for women in 2010).[1] Both Christian and secular bookshelves are filled with an array of books that lead us to "the one," and the media for young and old (consider Disney) tell us that we find completion in monogamous relationships. Being *outside* of a relationship, in both the church and in society, is considered somehow "less than" being *in* one. Author and columnist Camerin Courtney writes about idolizing marriage: "I'm not sure how or when marriage became the mark of an 'okay' human being, or, more important, how we singles accepted it as the mark of an okay human being. When I started looking at how I'd allowed myself to be lulled into this thinking, I saw subtle yet flawed reasons, many of which surprised me and most of which vanished when I brought them to the light."[2]

Several years ago, I was invited to speak at a session for college seniors who were preparing for the "next stage" of their lives. As usual, I had a whole chat planned on my assigned topic of singleness, with great encouragement to offer about living well as a single person. And yet, as I sat in the room, I was overcome with emotion, and felt the Lord calling me to change my chat. When I stood before the group, some of whom I knew well and some of whom I did not, my main point was that there is nothing wrong with you if you remain single for a while. There were tears in my eyes as I passionately told my audience that if they got married, it was because God loved them, and if they were single, it was because God loved them. It was not because there was some flaw that kept them from being married (it's not like all the married people we know are perfect, anyway). My words to them were also words from the Lord to my single self.

Singleness is not a curse for the faithless or an excuse for immaturity. It is simply a state of being unmarried, and there is nothing wrong with those who are single. In fact, if you know someone who was single a while before she married, she could easily tell you what she misses about being single; I know I could. Though I wanted a life partner in my many single years, I am grateful that I had a chance to learn to enjoy being single and realize myself as a complete person without a partner. Deciding to embrace my journey was key, and Courtney agrees:

> What baffles me is that those of us who are "still single" seem
> to be given a harder time as we hold out for a right, one-time-
> only marriage. We don't just want a marriage; we want a fulfilling,

1. US Census.
2. Courtney, *Table for One*, 20.

God-honoring life—whatever that may look like. That's the most difficult—though much more rewarding—path. And frankly, that's the path we deserve, the one Jesus spoke of when he said he came to this earth (from the glory of heaven, no less) to give us abundant life. I don't know about you, but I like the thought of an abundant life—much more so than a cookie-cutter kind of existence. And though it scared me to death, it wasn't until I was willing to embrace my singleness and dive whole-hog into this phase of life—not knowing if it would be five months, five years, five decades, or forever—that I finally discovered a truly happy, abundant life.[3]

Courtney was supposed to write *Table for One: The Savvy Girl's Guide to Singleness* with her friend Ginger, but Ginger got married before they got far and so disqualified herself as a coauthor. Courtney states that Ginger's marriage was great, but so was fulfilling her (Courtney's) own dream of becoming an author, because the point they wanted to make with the book was, "there's a whole lot more to life than one's marital status."[4] In fact, it is better to remain single than to rush into a hasty marriage with a less-than-ideal partner simply because one wants to get married.

We want to be interdependent, but as singles, our life goals and decisions are made mostly independently—this is both difficult and freeing. It's difficult because we make the decisions alone, but it's freeing because we can make decisions only thinking about ourselves rather than taking into account how the decisions affect a spouse or even children. Courtney writes, "I've watched friends get married because it was easier for them to walk down the aisle than to chart life's path or to dig deep and figure out just who God made them to be."[5] This is not to say that all who marry young are choosing an "easy path," but it is a temptation of which we can be aware.

Courtney's book has great, raw, and honest advice for living well as a single woman. As stated above, she writes how her friends are her family, and she recommends having four types of friends as a single woman: a married friend to keep us realistic and not movie-dreamy about romance and marriage, a guy friend to keep male presence in our lives "normal,"

3. Ibid., 21.
4. Ibid., 8.
5. Ibid., 114.

a sympathizer who intuitively knows how we feel (especially the negative emotions) without judging, and a cheerleader who celebrates us.[6]

Though while I was single, I found people's well-meaning question "Do you think you have the gift of celibacy?" rather annoying, I do look back and see my single years—years of travel, friends, adventure, dating— as a gift. They were a gift as all of life is a gift. It is my job to further my personal contentment and joy by being grateful for the gifts and enjoying what God brings into my life, whether single or married.

Besides, single theologian and prolific author John Piper gave a sermon based on Isaiah 56:1–7 entitled "Single in Christ: A Name Better than Sons and Daughters." He states, "My main point is that God promises those of you who remain single in Christ blessings that are better than the blessings of marriage and children, and he calls you to display, by the Christ-exalting devotion of your singleness, the truths about Christ and his kingdom that shine more clearly through singleness than through marriage and childrearing."[7] The truths to which he refers include:

- God's family grows through regeneration, not procreation

- Relationships in Christ are the most permanent

- Marriage is temporary

- Faith in Christ is paramount[8]

It is freeing to realize that as part of the kingdom of God, our commission is for *spiritual* procreation, the preaching of the gospel and discipling of believers (the Great Commission, Matt 28:19–20). It is not the same as the commission in Genesis to *physically* procreate, which we do in marriage.

Marriage is also not the only way to understand God's love, for it is an exclusive relationship. When we are married, we can no longer include others in the same way as before marriage. But God's love is not *only* exclusive. God also inclusively loves humankind, and singleness reflects that love. "Christianity makes this exclusive faith claim: Jesus is the only way of salvation. If we elevate marriage (also an exclusive relationship) as the only picture of God's love for the Church, we diminish the inclusive, universal, unencumbered love God has for all people."[9]

---

6. Ibid., 88–90.

7. Piper, "Single in Christ."

8. Ibid.

9. McMinn, *Sexuality and Holy Longing*, 69.

Marriage is not a reward for the faithful, a ticket to maturity, a remedy for anything, or the biblical choice for Christians. In fact, Paul encourages celibacy for its undivided devotion to Christ (1 Cor 7). When we think about the coming kingdom, it is a place where marriage no longer occurs. "Marriage [as it reflects Christ's relationship with the church] instructs the church in what to look for when the kingdom comes—eternal, intimate union. And singleness prepares us for the other piece of the end of time, the age when singleness trumps marriage. Singleness tutors us in our primary, heavenly relationship with one another: sibling in Christ."[10] May we learn to be skilled at our primary relationship as siblings in Christ, remembering that both singleness and marriage are good.

I always think it interesting to remember that the best, most self-actualized and impactful human in the history of the world, Jesus Christ, was single, according to historic Christianity. None of us see Jesus as somehow incomplete or lacking in his singleness, but we continue to receive much because of his service and sacrifice for the world. Therefore, let us not see ourselves or others lacking, either.

I was engaged at thirty-eight, married at thirty-nine, pregnant at forty, and am now expecting my first child after I turn forty-one. I was recently reflecting about my single years, and wrote this to a friend:

> You're on my mind this morning, friend. I'm sitting here thinking about how many weddings I'm invited to this summer and how you're choosing not to always go to the ones you're invited to as I did for a time. I'm praying for you.
>
> I'm also sitting here married and pregnant. I don't say that to brag. I'm simply being thankful and remembering that there were many years that I thought this would never happen. I think I wasted time mourning its seeming impossibility. It was really hard, but I really think I wasted time on it. Often I forgot to be thankful for what I had, to enjoy life as it was, to choose happiness. I was in pain, true, but I chose to wallow in it rather than to find my joy and wallow in that. I worried.
>
> Now, I can't guarantee your future family, but you and I have seen several women in their thirties marry. So, it happens. Let it happen (for you), but in the meantime, love your life. Don't concentrate on marriage so much that it overshadows your great joys and accomplishments. Love your life as it is. I'm proud of you.

10. Winner, *Real Sex*, 147.

To chat about over tea, coffee, and/or chocolate:

Are you single? Are you happy with it?

What is your attitude toward singleness (for yourself and others) and how do the ideas written here affect it?

What goals are you pursuing with regard to your relationships with others?

Prayer

O, Trinitarian God who is forever in community, grant that I may be so transformed into your image that I may fellowship in community as you are in community. Show me myself so that I can bring her to others; empower me to be like Jesus in relationships, and guide me into interdependence. Empower me to resist sexual temptation and guide me into friendships and partnerships with men. Teach me to embrace and love my life, whether single, dating, or married. As Jesus heals, please heal relational areas in my life that need it; as the Holy Spirit leads, please lead me into relationships that are glorifying to you in all ways; and as the Father parents, please bring me mentors, spiritual mothers and fathers that will nurture and challenge me. May I be so transformed that I am able to bless and bring wholeness to the people of this broken world. I pray this in the name of the Son, to the glory of the Father, and by the power of the Holy Spirit.

Amen.

13

First Comes Love . . .

The Dating Life

It took a long time, but I've finally figured it out. When it comes to men who are romantically interested in you, it's really simple. Just ignore everything they say and only pay attention to what they do.

~ RANDY PAUSCH, *THE LAST LECTURE*

Love is like a virus. It can happen to anybody at any time.

~ MAYA ANGELOU, GLOBAL RENAISSANCE WOMAN

He's so lucky to be going out with me.

~ KATE MIDDLETON, DUCHESS OF CAMBRIDGE

IN MY THEOLOGY CLASSES, our discussion on men and women usually begins with my "bad date" story. I tell them about the youth pastor one of my students set me up with the first year I taught college. Our third date finds us at Macaroni Grill, where, as you may have experienced, you write on the paper-covered tables with crayons. I busily sign my name, "Amy F. Davis," and when he looks at it, he laughs.

"Fanny," he says, "I'll bet everyone called you 'Fanny' growing up!" If you are unaware, "fanny" is not only a euphemism for one's derriere, but also a nickname for Frances, which is, in fact, my middle name. I look up at him, a bit offended, and wanting to turn the tide of the conversation, I state, "Frances is actually my middle name. I was named after my grandmother, and after she passed, I started signing the 'F' in the middle of my name."

Unfazed, he continues, "That's great. How about you start honoring someone *after* they're dead. What does it matter to them? Unless they're looking down from the sky at you!" Now, I look at him hard, with tears in my eyes, "You're messing with something sacred, and you need to stop." At this point, I should have said, "Take me home now," but was not that assertive in my younger days.

After his apology, we order, and sometime during the meal, he states, "All women should submit to all men." I state that Scripture (in the English translation)[1] only states that wives should submit to their husbands. However, governing the entire passage is a phrase that Paul puts writes first, "Submit to *one another* out of reverence for Christ" (Eph 5:21, emphasis added).

He says, "That passage isn't at the beginning, it's at the end!" Since smartphones don't yet exist, I challenge him to check it at the Barnes and Noble down the hall after we finish. When we do, I show him that it is at the beginning, but he says, "Yeah, just like *I* said!"

Needless to say, we did not go out again.

Though dating is supposed to be fun and often is, it is also sometimes not done well, as my example shows. The students and I always laugh at the experience, but when it actually happened, I did not find it amusing. I haven't discovered as many good books about dating as there are about marriage and parenting. While not all will marry or become a parent, many will date, break up, and date again.

After a particularly painful breakup, an acquaintance gave me Neil Clark Warren's *Finding the Love of Your Life: Ten Principles for Choosing the Right Marriage Partner*. My shelf already had *The Idiot's Guide to Understanding Men and Women*, as well as Elisabeth Elliot's classic, *Passion and Purity*. During that time of singleness, I enlarged the shelf with *Men are From Mars, Women are From Venus*; *The Five Love Languages: How to Express Heartfelt Commitment to Your Mate*; and *Boundaries in Dating: How Healthy Choices Grow Healthy Relationships*. Another favorite that was turned into a movie was *He's Just Not That Into You: The No-Excuses Truth*

---

1. The word *submit* is not in the Greek original in Ephesians 5:22.

To Understanding Guys, in which Greg Behrendt and Liz Tuccillo try to stop women from staying with or chasing men who aren't all that interested.

And finally, I have *All the Rules: Time-Tested Secrets for Capturing the Heart of Mr. Right,* a somewhat controversial best seller with suggestions that seem a bit manipulative. However, the back cover states, "The goal? Marriage, in the shortest time possible, to a man you love, who loves you even more than you love him. Whether you're eighteen or eighty, a beauty queen or a woman with ordinary looks, *THE RULES* will work for you."[2] Both Christian and secular, these books are just a sampling of the relationship books that exist.[3]

Kathleen Bogle's recent work, *Hooking Up: Sex, Dating, and Relationships on Campus,* shed much-needed light on how the world of male-female relationships has drastically changed in the last sixty years. In the past, people would casually date, going to dinner, for ice cream, or a movie with no ensuing sexual contact, and if a woman wasn't "going steady" with a boy, she could date several men at once. Today, rather than dating, Bogle shows that college students tend to socialize and party in groups. At the parties, it is common for those attracted to one another to "hook up," to have some type of sexual encounter. Hooking up could mean anything from kissing to sexual intercourse, and she found that it was only after a couple had hooked up several times that they might actually go out on dates and be in an "official" relationship. After college, people actually date, and for many from the hookup culture, it is a strange experience.[4]

The Christian college campus is not immune to the hookup scene, and "hanging out" tends to happen more than dating, leaving people confused and unsure of whether their time spent with the opposite sex is a friendship or something "more." Joshua Harris did not address hooking up, but he did encourage Christians to "Kiss Dating Goodbye," embrace old-style courtship, and only pursue marriage.[5] Christians are caught between a world where casual sexual "hookups" are commonplace and an ancient world where marriage is the primary goal of male-female relationships and no hooking up or even dating occurs before marriage is on the table.

2. Fein and Schneider, *All the Rules.*

3. Having all of these titles in my list does not signify wholehearted endorsement of them.

4. Bogle, *Hooking Up.*

5. Harris, *I Kissed Dating Goodbye.*

Talk of "emotional purity" as well as "sexual purity" for many Christian college students means not dating at all until they have found "the one" they desire to marry. This obviously puts overwhelming pressure on dating, resulting in women waiting and waiting for a man to initiate, and according to one student, if asked out, "they think, 'We have to make this work. I might not get asked out for another 10 years.'"[6] And perchance two students date, it is never a casual date or two, but always begins as a relationship.[7]

Though this may seem too pressurized, it is a cycle that few know how to avoid. Many Christians advise actually dating and avoiding hooking up, but with a few twists that distinguish it from the common Christian pressurized relationship-only dating. Contrary to what some believe, the ideal life is not to date only one person ever, and then marry him. Though that may be God's plan for the couple that does it, clearly it is not God's plan for everyone. Embracing our own journeys and dating well requires not comparing our journey to others' and living life as it comes to us.

According to Cloud and Townsend, who encourage dating, Joshua Harris thought dating should be "kissed goodbye" because it was too painful. While Cloud and Townsend agree that the pain must stop, they blame the pain on people rather than on dating. "In the same way that cars don't kill people, drunk drivers do, dating does not hurt people, but dating in out-of-control ways does."[8] Even as they agree that some people should not date, at least for a while, they also think that dating is beneficial because:

1. Dating gives people the opportunity to learn about themselves, others, and relationships in a safe context [the safe context is caring community] . . .

2. Dating provides a context to work through issues . . .

3. Dating helps build relationship skills . . .

4. Dating can heal and repair . . .

5. Dating is relational and has value in and of itself . . .

6. Dating lets someone learn what he or she likes in the opposite sex . . .

7. Dating gives a context to learn sexual self-control and other delays of gratification. . .[9]

6. Olasky, "Christian Boy Meets Christian Girl."

7. Ibid.

8. Cloud and Townsend, *Boundaries in Dating*, 10–11.

9. Ibid., 17–21.

Personally, in my time of dating, I experienced pain, but I also experienced all of the above benefits.

Too often, the primary question is *whether or not* we are dating. This, however, is not the best question to ask. Cloud and Townsend recommend asking, "Who are you in your dating and who are you becoming in your dating? What is the fruit of your dating for you and for the people that you date? How are you treating them? What are you learning?"[10] I know while I dated, I tended to be more concerned with whether the relationship would last than with what I was learning, the fruit of the dating for me, and who I was becoming. God did not answer my prayer requesting that I only be in a relationship with the man I would marry, because God had other plans for my dating life. Successful dating in God's eyes is not about walking down the aisle, but rather about being conformed into God's image whatever the outcome.

After realizing this truth, I began to pray differently—I prayed that God would allow the relationship to end once I had given and received all God wanted me to give and receive in the relationship. That allowed me to concentrate more on the process and on our growth as people than on my goal of marriage.

Not that I always dated smoothly, but I think my attitude in dating matured as time went on. Most have experienced that dating is not all "bells and roses"—there are difficulties!

> Simply put, many of the struggles people experience in dating relationships are, at the heart, *caused by some problems in the areas of freedom and responsibility.* By freedom, we mean your ability to make choices based on your values, rather than choosing out of fear or guilt. Free people make commitments because they feel it's the right thing to do, and they are wholehearted about it. By responsibility, we mean your ability to execute your tasks in keeping the relationship healthy and loving, as well as being able to say no to things you shouldn't be responsible for. Responsible people shoulder their part of the dating relationship, but they don't tolerate harmful or inappropriate behavior.[11]

We want to be free—to freely make personally authentic choices, and to be responsible—to responsibly say "yes" and "no" with our voices and actions. Cloud and Townsend's helpful text defines this further, encouraging us to

10. Ibid., 11.

11. Ibid., 27; emphasis original.

make boundaries, or property lines, that protect our own soul.[12] This advice is apropos to any relationship, not just dating relationships.

McMinn states that one of the unintended consequences of dating is that a power differential exists—the men have the power to ask, and the women are supposed to wait and be flirtatious, sometimes seductive, but always indirect.[13] This power differential, among other negative consequences, can contribute to date rape. McMinn suggests that in order to fight the power differential, the woman can pay her own way and even initiate activities with men.[14] This makes women an equal partner in the relationship, and I have had several happily married female friends who initiated the relationship with their spouses; one simply stated on the phone, "I think I like you for more than a friend," and then hung up, while the other asked him out on a casual date.

Nicole Unice wrote an article in *Relevant Magazine* that asked the question "How Should Christians Date?" and proposed several ways to date like "normal people"—not immediately pursuing marriage, and not simply "hanging out." First, we can date indiscriminately by spending specific time with people that are interesting, realizing that the commitment is not marriage, but rather a few hours, and is simply an opportunity to get to know others.[15] In my dating days, it was seldom that I was asked out, so whenever I was, I would say "yes" as long as I was not putting myself in any danger. I would also often go out on more than one date before I decided I was or wasn't interested. Dating can be fun when we choose to shed the pressure.

Unice also proposed that we date casually, since we can't really get to know people in group settings the same way we know people one-on-one, and to date often, since we need the practice. She cites her husband's thirty-eight job interviews as a reminder that he got better at answering questions and explaining himself as he kept doing interviews. We get better at dating and being in relationships with more practice.

Finally, she also suggests making the first five dates a time to get to know someone without thinking about a future with him.[16] I think her advice is both timely and wise. And if we follow Cloud and Towsend's advice,

12. Ibid., 28–30.

13. McMinn, *Growing Strong Daughters,* 153.

14. Ibid., 156.

15. Unice, "How Should Christians Date?"

16. Ibid.

too, we will be able to begin and sometimes end dating relationships respectfully and well.

So, as far as it depends on you, choose to date well. Only one of your dating relationships will end in marriage, but when you are careful and wise, dating can be fun and a way of getting to know people, which also helps you to know yourself!

Some dating relationships lead to marriage, a state different from all other relationships described here, though many of the same principles are still useful. Tomes have been written on marriage, including another *Boundaries* book by Cloud and Townsend. While many readers of this book may find themselves married and with children, I recommend finding books specifically on those subjects to help in those relationships.

Since we are created in the image of God, we are inherently relational, and as we know ourselves and bring her to others, Jesus' life presents a fantastic example to follow in our relationships. Whether our relationships are with female peers, older or younger women, or with men, we can carefully and wisely live out these relationships with the power of the Holy Spirit.

I often state that any meeting we have with another person is an opportunity to enter their story. In each interaction we have the opportunity to do one of three things—to bless, to do nothing, or to curse. Others can walk away from our brief part in their story feeling better, the same, or worse. As Christian women we have the opportunity to contribute to healing in the area of relationships in this world through blessing others. We can make it a goal in our relationships with others to partner with God in bringing about the healing of the brokenness in the world, an act that will transform many of our relationships from serving ourselves to serving others.

To chat about over tea, coffee, and/or chocolate:

Do you date? What have your experiences been like, and how will the advice here help transform it?

What boundaries, or property lines that protect your own soul, are important in your dating relationships?

How do you understand purity?

What goals are you pursuing with regard to your relationships with others?

Prayer

O, Trinitarian God who is forever in community, grant that I may be so transformed into your image that I may fellowship in community as you are in community. Show me myself so that I can bring her to others; make me to be like Jesus in relationships, and guide me into interdependence. Empower me to resist sexual temptation and guide me into friendships, partnerships, and dating relationships with men. Teach me to embrace and love my life, whether single, dating, or married. As Jesus heals, please heal relational areas in my life that need it; as the Holy Spirit leads, please lead me into relationships that are glorifying to you in all ways; and as the Father parents, please bring me mentors, spiritual mothers and fathers that will nurture and challenge me. May I be so transformed that I am able to bless and bring wholeness to the people of this broken world. I pray this in the name of the Son, to the glory of the Father, and by the power of the Holy Spirit.

Amen.

SECTION FOUR

Relationship with Creation

"I gained a new appreciation for creation and saw how it really is
a part of our identity and needs to be cared for."

"I think the fact that I think twice about the length of my showers and
how much meat I eat is a significant change that has occurred for me since
Woman. Also, Sabbath is awesome. Rest is awesome. Rejuvenation is awesome. I realized, through working on my project, that I enjoy being creative.
I should seek to do it often because it brings me peace and a chance to let
some things out."

"Sabbaths are essential and my creativity doesn't
have to look like anyone else's!"

Introduction

Nature-Like

"Blessed women of God, you have come to develop your relationship with creation. In your survey, you answered questions regarding your care of the earth that God has entrusted to you, and now we journey together, agreeing with creational rest through practicing Sabbath, devoting ourselves not only to other humans, but to the world God has given to us, caring for the earth in the ways available to us, exploring our creativity, and seeking to steward the earth in a way that opens possibilities for a richer life for all. We welcome you."

"I HATE NATURE!" SHE cried vehemently and loudly. At first, I was taken aback. Having grown up in upstate New York with a backyard that had a little bit of grass before the woods, and a shaded front yard with a small creek by the road, I couldn't imagine truly hating nature. Every summer I would run around barefoot, dance in the rain and mud, play with my toy boat in the creek, and desperately need a bath before bedtime. Summer family vacations consisted of long drives to the western United States, camping sometimes primitively and sometimes with flush toilets and showers, hiking, rock hounding, spelunking, and using all my senses to explore the beautiful world around me. If someone wants to truly know me, they need to hike with me and see my legs leap like a mountain goat's, gaze at a waterfall with me, or otherwise explore with me. My deep love and ingrained regard for all that inhabits the outdoors was in stark contrast to my friend's hatred of it.

Though I couldn't understand how anyone could hate nature, I know that my friend is not alone. I have heard many echoes of her statement from others, albeit they were not always as clear and strong. For that reason, I know that this portion of *Woman* can be intimidating to those who have never really liked the world out-of-doors. Participants wonder if someone will force them to go on a hike, or plant seeds, or jump in the leaves, or hug a tree, or otherwise involve themselves in the dirt that is always a part of outdoor activities. Relationship with God, self, and others make sense, but with creation? "Is that last one really necessary?" they ask.

Allow me a moment to assuage your fears. No one will be forced to become a tree hugger, and though I may invite you on a hike, I will not make you love creation the way I do. Relationship with creation includes all that we see outside our window, but it also encompasses our Sabbath rhythm, conservation that makes a difference to people in the world, and creativity in any way we can express it. We want to have a broad and full relationship with creation that includes all of this—Sabbath, conservation, and creativity—not one that is limited to a love for birds and trees.

Back to the Beginning

We need to go back to the beginning to understand the importance of one's relationship with creation. As with nearly all our ideas, our theology of creation is rooted in Genesis, in humans being creatures in the midst of other creatures yet distinct because we are created in the image of God.

First, let us consider the word, *creation*, a word we will prefer over *nature*. In Genesis we see that God created, and in whatever way one interprets *how* that occurred, it is clear that God *had* and *has* a lot to do with the world that we see around us, as well as with ourselves. To call the world around us "nature" can depersonalize it, making it "that stuff" rather than living things that originated with a living, loving God. "Creation" reminds us that God creates beautifully and broadly, and the word makes what we see more personal.

Using the term *creation* forms a world view that assumes creation is "unable to exist by itself and so must be sustained by a *Creator*."[1] It also allows us to see ourselves as "*creatures*, things made and existing with other creatures in the world, all for the purposes and pleasures of God."[2] Saying

1. Van Dyke et al., *Redeeming Creation*, 40; emphasis original.
2. Ibid., emphasis original.

"creation" reminds us of our need for the Creator and Sustainer, and places us in communion with others and God.

God created, and since we are in the image of God, we also create. In the first chapter, we realized that the term *image* was reminiscent of the images of the rulers that were placed in the various cities of the empire. As such images, we represent the benevolent, caring, beautiful ruling of God over creation. We are like God and we represent God. We are created for relationship and stewardship of creation, all of which God called good.

At a retreat that sought to define secularization, we tried to place certain ideas, actions, or objects in the categories of either "sacred" or "secular." I stated the idea, action, or object, and participants moved from one side of the room to the other, depending on whether they thought it was sacred or secular. As one might imagine, there were a variety of opinions of the sacredness or secularity of ideas such as music, sexual intercourse, science, the body, etc. If I had thought of it, I would have liked to see whether people thought creation to be secular or sacred. Perhaps, simply by using the word *creation* over *nature*, we point to its sacredness.

Honestly, I think that nature *is* sacred, simply because God created it and called it good. I think of myself as sacred for the same reason, and because *I* am sacred, what I do is also sacred. There is no secular/sacred binary for me or for my actions. My identity as sacred spills over into my actions.

I read Lisa Graham McMinn's book *The Contented Soul* not because I *am* always a contented soul, but because I *want* to be one, to live contentedly as Paul describes: "I have learned the secret of being content in any and every situation, whether well fed or hungry, whether living in plenty or in want. I can do all this through him who gives me strength" (Phil 4:12–13). I realize that it may take time to *learn* "the secret of being content," but I want to take that time, because I think it demonstrates trust in God, which brings us peace. McMinn connects an understanding of the sacredness of creation to contentment. "A characteristic I observe in contented souls is a tendency to define creation as sacred, bringing an obligation and expectation that they treat it with respect and care. Contentment and care for creation are interwoven strands emerging from who we are: image bearers of God and dust of the earth . . . . Contentment is a by-product of living rightly, properly understanding our obligatory relationship to creation."[3]

3. McMinn, *The Contented Soul*, 125.

Because we are in the image of God, we can see personal sacredness as well as the sacredness of the creation. I am not suggesting that we think of creation as divine, for it is not. Although God may be seen in creation, God is not creation. We as God's representatives are called to steward sacred creation.

Even though we may think of ourselves as sacred, many Christians still ignore any sacredness in creation. Rather than seeing themselves as creatures among other creatures, they see themselves as high above creation and licensed to use creation however they desire or see fit. As those in God's image, though, we are intrinsically relational and called to stewardship of creation. "The creation is God's, and has been entrusted to humanity, who is to act as its steward, not its exploiter."[4] May we be those whose relationship with creation is not exploitative, but intentionally aware of its sacredness.

Not only does the image of God in us call us to relationship with creation, but it also calls us to create. God created beautifully, and because we bear the image of God, we create as well. I don't mean we can all paint or sing or play an instrument, but that we are able to be deeply and widely creative in any area or vocation we follow. Engineers are creative in the building of bridges and buildings, relief workers are creative in figuring out how to care for huge numbers of refugees, educators and pastors are creative in their communication; those at the top of their fields are all connected to their personal creativity and are able to daringly create, sometimes alone, but often with others. Creativity is inherent in each of us, though it has often been hidden because we narrowly define it. Not only are we called to care for creation, but we are also called to create with God-image creativity! We "are creative and able to create what is good and beautiful."[5]

4. McGrath, "The Stewardship of the Creation," 87.
5. McMinn, *Growing Strong Daughters*, 24.

14

The Rest of Creation

Sabbath

Nothing less than a command has the power to intervene in the vicious, ac-
celerating, self-perpetuating cycle of faithless and graceless busy-ness, the only
part of which we are conscious being our good intentions.

~ EUGENE PETERSON, PASTOR, SCHOLAR, AUTHOR

If we are not able to rest one day a week, we are taking ourselves far too seriously.

~ MARVA DAWN, THEOLOGIAN, AUTHOR, EDUCATOR

The spiritual rest which God especially intends in this commandment [to keep
the Sabbath holy] is that we not only cease from our labor and trade but much
more—that we let God alone work in us and that in all our powers we do nothing of our own.

~ MARTIN LUTHER, REFORMER

WE WILL SOON TURN to what it means to be involved in conservation and
how to access and use our creativity, but first, we will look at a spiritual discipline that reflects our relationship with creation: Sabbath. Sabbath, too,
is introduced in the beginning. "By the seventh day God had finished the

work he had been doing; so on the seventh day he rested from all his work. Then God blessed the seventh day and made it holy, because on it he rested from all the work of creating that he had done" (Gen 2:2–3). God completed the creation, and then rested; the final act was blessing that seventh day.

Many of us have different images when it comes to the word *Sabbath*. For some, since Jesus did not verbally repeat the command to honor the Sabbath day in the same way he repeated other commands, they do not think it is a binding command for Christians. For others, Sabbath is a still, severe day, void of laughter, meant for serious spiritual study or service. Still others think of Sabbath as joyful, but not a time to make others work or to go to the movies. We have very diverse views of Sabbath!

My Call to Sabbath

I was first introduced to Sabbath as a spiritual discipline during my initial semester in seminary. It was in a spiritual formation class, and I can even picture the room where our Old Testament professor stood up and called us to be Sabbath-honorers. I don't recall the full lecture, but I remember the inspiring thought that we rest because God is a finisher: so many tasks in our life will never be finished, but we rest because God completed creation; we rest to celebrate that God even completes work in us.

I was convinced.

But I also thought there was no way I could actually have one day a week when I did no regular work. I was a full-time student, working three jobs to stay ahead and out of debt. There was no time for rest, for if I rested, the work would not be completed. I figured that I had time each day when I "rested," whether it was getting coffee with a friend, or going for a walk or a run, so I decided that was sufficient. Weekends were spent primarily on reading and writing for classes. Though I was called, I did not make Sabbath my discipline.

Fast forward two years. Two years of hard work and study, two years of not receiving the Sabbath rest God had for me. I am doing an internship at a church in Florida. At that point, I plan to be in full-time church ministry for the rest of my life, and I realize that the habits I form *now* will likely follow me forever. I want to form good habits.

It is a multi-staffed church, and I notice that two of the people on staff have lives that seem to be characterized by joy and peace. My life is characterized by hard work, and I want more joy and peace. I soon learn that they are committed to the discipline of Sabbath. Friday is their day off, and they do no regular work—they rest in the finished work of God. Following them, I decide that my internship would be a great time to try that discipline to which I had been called several years before.

So, I do. Since Sunday is always a day of work for me, I choose my day off on Thursday to be Sabbath. I read Marva Dawn's *Keeping the Sabbath Wholly*, and falteringly begin. I light a cucumber-melon candle that I bought at the local flea market on Wednesday evening after I arrive home from work, and pray a traditional Sabbath-welcoming prayer. And then I do no regular work for the next twenty-four hours, burning the cucumber-melon candle only on Thursdays, and praying another prayer before I go to bed that night that thanks God for Sabbath.

A lover of planning, I plan little or nothing on this day. Sometimes I lounge at home and read on the lanai, sit in the sun or swim in the gulf, and at other times, I ride my bike around the island or to the coffee shop. When I think of work-related ideas or tasks, I write them down and lay them aside to think about on Friday. My goal is to cease worrying, controlling, and accomplishing. All of this stretches me.

And some Sabbaths are incredible times of resting in the grace of God.

And on others, I wake up grumpy, feel tired all day, and head to bed still in a sour mood.

Either way, I do it. I agree with the wisdom and gift of Sabbath.

Sabbath in the Bible

During that time, I learn a lot about Sabbath, a concept I'd never been taught. Jesus' idea of Sabbath was not to reject it as some think, but to understand it well, something the scribes and Pharisees had not accomplished. The Pharisees had a habit of building a fence around the law—as if the law God gave needed to be protected so that the people would not get close enough to break it. To fence its perimeter, they added specific rules to the law to make sure it wasn't broken; in the case of Sabbath, they sought to specifically and narrowly define the "work" that was not to be done. In so doing, they missed the heart of the law, and that's why Jesus confronted them about Sabbath. The heart of the law is only found by correctly interpreting the Hebrew Bible's references to Sabbath.

Hebrew Bible Sabbath

Keeping the Sabbath day holy is a command, the fourth in the list of ten. Thus, it is written in both Exodus 20 and Deuteronomy 5 with all the others. Exodus 20 states,

> Remember the Sabbath day by keeping it holy. Six days you shall labor and do all your work, but the seventh day is a Sabbath to the Lord your God. On it you shall not do any work, neither you, nor your son or daughter, nor your male or female servant, nor your animals, nor any foreigner residing in your towns. For in six days the Lord made the heavens and the earth, the sea, and all that is in them, but he rested on the seventh day. Therefore the Lord blessed the Sabbath day and made it holy (verses 8–11).

In this case, no one was supposed to do any work on Sabbath—the Israelites were not to work, and they were not to make anyone else work, either. The reason given here is that God did it. We honor and celebrate Sabbath to do what God did when God rested.

Deuteronomy 5 sounds similar, but has a particular distinctive:

> Observe the Sabbath day by keeping it holy, as the Lord your God has commanded you. Six days you shall labor and do all your work, but the seventh day is a Sabbath to the Lord your God. On it you shall not do any work, neither you, nor your son or daughter, nor your male or female servant, nor your ox, your donkey or any of your animals, nor any foreigner residing in your towns, so that your male and female servants may rest, as you do. Remember that you were slaves in Egypt and that the Lord your God brought you out of there with a mighty hand and an outstretched arm. Therefore the Lord your God has commanded you to observe the Sabbath day (verses 12–15).

Here, the reason to rest is that the Israelites are no longer slaves. Deuteronomy is introduced as Moses's sermons on the plains of Moab before the people enter the promised land. Slavery in Egypt was not far back in their history; their relatives had told them what it was like to be slaves. They were to rest as free people because God brought them out of slavery. Slaves don't get to decide when to work and when to rest; they do what they are told. However, these people were free, and were able to honor God and their freedom by resting on Sabbath.

Let's take a step back from both of these commandments and think about what we see here. Both these commands assume six days of working.

This is not a command to be lazy or otherwise shirk responsibility, but rather, one rests after working for six days. And one rests to do what God did and to celebrate freedom. Like the Israelites who were once slaves to the Egyptians, we Christians were once slaves to sin. Now we are free to be slaves to righteousness, and we celebrate that freedom on Sabbath. It is a weekly reminder of our identity as saints who sometimes sin.

Another key passage about Sabbath in the Pentateuch is Leviticus 25. This chapter is about the Sabbath year and the year of Jubilee. The people are to work the fields for six years, yet on the seventh year,

> The land is to have a year of Sabbath rest, a Sabbath to the Lord. Do not sow your fields or prune your vineyards. Do not reap what grows of itself or harvest the grapes of your untended vines. The land is to have a year of rest. Whatever the land yields during the Sabbath year will be food for you—for yourself, your male and female servants, and the hired worker and temporary resident who live among you, as well as for your livestock and the wild animals in your land. Whatever the land produces may be eaten (verses 4–7).

Here, the people are commanded to end the work not for one day of respite, but for an entire year. They weren't to hoard everything from previous years to prepare for this, but they were simply to rest and allow the land to rest.

I did not grow up on a farm, but my mother did. And she told me how on the farm, the work never ended. For a people who depend on their crops to live, this command of a year of rest would take a significant amount of trust in God to provide everything they needed. They would have to assume that if God is truly sovereign and that their obedience to this God would not cause them to die, but to live well. Some think that this was simply a command to rotate crops, an action that has been proven to enrich and enliven the soil. God was simply commanding that they leave individual, smaller plots fallow every seven years so that plot would be able to produce even more. However, if this were the case, I think the Scripture would have stated it more clearly; as it is, it sounds like they were to stop it *all* for a year.

And, believe it or not, that's not everything. Not only do they give the land Sabbath for a year, but when they make it to the seventh of seven years, the forty-ninth year, they were to proclaim the fiftieth year as a year of Jubilee, a year when they did not plant *again*. Imagine that—two whole years without planting! Now, many other freedoms were to occur on that fiftieth year, but we will concentrate simply on the agricultural rest.

What would it take for me, if I were a farmer, to not plant for two years in a row? It would take a huge amount of trust that neither I nor my family would go hungry. I would no longer trust in myself to feed them, but I would completely trust Almighty God to take care of us. God would have to provide food for us, though I was not working.

This complete trust, my friends, is the key to Sabbath. It's about choosing to trust in God, not in ourselves. It's about realizing that we are free, and trusting God to keep us so. It's about awareness of all our unfinished work in the world, remembering that God is the finisher who completes the work, and resting, trusting that God will complete *our* work, too.

At the end of the day, I think the primary question of the Christian life is whether we trust God or not. I celebrate a weekly Sabbath to remind me to choose to trust God as finisher, completer, and as my freedom. I'm not always good at trusting—that's evident in my struggles against anxiety—but Sabbath helps me practice trusting. It also brings even greater freedom to my life.

Before we leave the Hebrew Bible, one question is unanswered: how did they do? Did they ever truly honor this Sabbath day *and* Sabbath year? We don't think so. When the people of the kingdom of Judah were taken into exile in Babylon, 2 Chronicles 36:21 states that the land enjoyed its Sabbath rests. It rested for the seventy years that Judah was supposed to give it rest but chose not to. They tended to trust in themselves rather than God, and the outcome was exile. God still gave the land what it needed, the rest they had refused to give it.

> "Sabbath is very important and is a part of self-care and trusting in God."

New Testament Sabbath

In the New Testament, Jesus is a Sabbath-honorer, but the Pharisees don't like the way he does it. Jesus, however, knew the heart of the law, not just its outward rules like the Pharisees. Somehow, in the mind-set of the Pharisees, healing was included in the work that was prohibited on Sabbath. And Jesus healed. On Sabbath. Several times. In Luke 13, Jesus heals a woman that had been crippled for eighteen years, and the synagogue leader responds, "There are six days for work. So come and be healed on those days, not on the Sabbath" (Luke 13:14). Jesus replies to his rebuke by calling him (and those who agreed with him) hypocrites because they "work" on Sabbath by untying their animals and leading them to food and drink. He rhetorically asks whether this woman could not also be "untied" from what had bound her for eighteen years.

Jesus heals the crippled man at the pool on Sabbath (John 5:1–14), he heals the man born blind on Sabbath (John 9), and he heals the man with the shriveled hand on Sabbath (Matt 12:1–14, Mark 2:23—3:6, and Luke 6:1–11). Jesus points out the hypocrisy and double standards of the Pharisees by asserting that it is lawful to do good on the Sabbath.

Jesus also calls himself Lord of the Sabbath in this latter instance, meaning that he, not the Pharisees, is able to define what Sabbath means. Furthermore, he states that Sabbath is made as a gift for us; we aren't made to be slaves to it (Mark 2:27). Jesus correctly interprets the Sabbath, and WWJD? He would celebrate Sabbath!

Lauren Winner, Orthodox Jew converted to Protestantism, states that Sabbath is what she misses most about Judaism. She describes what to do on that day: "You are commanded, principally, to be joyful and restful on Shabbat, to hold great feasts, sing happy hymns, dress in your finest. Married couples even get rabbinical brownie points for having sex on the Sabbath."[1] Sabbath is made for joy and feasting, not for seriousness and study. Orthodox Jews spend Sabbath "creating nothing, destroying nothing, and enjoying the bounty of the earth."[2]

What follows are two Jewish perspectives on Sabbath that can be added to the Christian perspectives that begin this chapter. Take a few moments to ponder their words of wisdom:

> The meaning of the Sabbath is to celebrate time rather than space. Six days a week we live under the tyranny of things of space; on the Sabbath we try to become attuned to holiness in time. It is a day on which we are called upon to share in what is eternal in time, to turn from the results of creation to the mystery of creation; from the world of creation to the creation of the world.
> ~ ABRAHAM JOSHUA HESCHEL[3]

> What happens when we stop working and controlling nature? When we don't operate machines or pick flowers, or pluck fish from the sea? . . . When we cease interfering in the world we are acknowledging that it is God's world.
> ~ MOSHE KONIGSBERG[4]

1. Winner, *Mudhouse Sabbath*, 4–5.
2. Van Dyke et al., *Redeeming Creation*, 67.
3. Heschel, *The Sabbath*, 10.
4. Quoted in Harris, *Holy Days*, 68–69.

My Story

> "Sabbath has been the best thing that ever existed!"

As for me, I started "Sabbathing" that summer when I was in Florida. I liked it. I found myself more rested and trusting of God. At times, I would work late on Wednesdays just to allow the next day to be empty, and this was great for me.

It was one thing to do it there, though, where I was able to reinvent myself to a certain extent. When I return to seminary that fall is when I really feel that Sabbath will be tested. I am still a full-time student, still working three jobs to keep afloat, and I'm not sure that Sabbath will allow me to function well in this environment. Since I'm not working on Sundays, I choose Sunday as Sabbath because it also incorporates corporate worship, an important aspect of Sabbath.

I basically pray, "God, I'm doing this because I'm seeking to be obedient to you." I figure both celebrating Sabbath and being a student are God's will in my life, so they have to somehow work together.

I am amazed.

I complete all my work on time.

And in the middle of October, I not only do not work on Sunday, I also have no work to do on one Monday. I go for a long hike in the woods and get a little lost, but that's another story.

> "Sabbath is very important and is a part of self-care and trusting in God."

Lauren Winner points out that while we may become more productive (as I experienced) as we celebrate Sabbath, productivity is not the purpose, but is at odds with the spirit of Sabbath.[5] We rest because we are commanded to, we follow God's example, we are not slaves, and most importantly because we want to show that we trust in God.

So, I challenge you to be Sabbath-honorers. I challenge you to rest one day a week and show that you trust in God, not yourself. Indeed, it may be difficult at first, you may have to start slowly, and you may be afraid that some things just won't get done. Though in my personal experience I got it all done, I chose *not* to do some things in order to allow for Sabbath in my life. Perhaps we can consider that if God calls us to Sabbath, and if we

---

5. Winner, *Mudhouse Sabbath*, 7.

are doing too much to accomplish it all in the six other days, maybe God's *not* calling us to all that we have on our plate. I think God prepares us to accomplish what God has called us to. The last thirteen years of being a Sabbath-honorer have brought great joy, peace, and trust in my life.

And because God rests on Sabbath in creation, we are simply agreeing with the rhythm that is inherent in us. As image-bearers, we rest as God rested. We agree with the need, like all creation, for work and rest (consider how the trees show us this work and rest in seasons). This develops a greater relationship with creation for us. In his book, *The Creation*, Trophime Mouiren writes, "The creation has no meaning for [people] unless [a person] takes time to give it meaning in rest and prayer: rest in order to look at the world otherwise than simply as answering his needs; prayer, to ask God's blessings, to offer something to God."[6]

To chat about over tea, coffee, and/or chocolate:

Are you a Sabbath-honorer? Why or why not?

What do you think about the reasons to celebrate Sabbath? If you are inspired to start, how do you plan to do so?

How is your relationship with the outdoor world?

Prayer

Almighty and most gracious God, I praise you for your creation is fearful and wonderful. I also declare that you are the trustworthy God who is always worthy of my actions and attitude of trust. Teach me to be a Sabbath-honorer. Transform my heart to understand how I am a creature in the midst of creation. I want to live to praise you. In the name of the Father, the Son, and the Holy Spirit, One God, forever and ever.

Amen.

6. As quoted in Van Dyke et al., *Redeeming Creation*, 67.

15

Back to Earth

Conservation

It is not possible to love an unseen God while mistreating God's visible creation.

~ JOHN WOOLMAN, EIGHTEENTH-CENTURY QUAKER
ABOLITIONIST

Recall that whatever lofty things you might accomplish today, you will do them
only because you first ate something that grew out of dirt.

~ BARBARA KINGSOLVER, AUTHOR

You can tell how high a society is by how much of its garbage is recycled.

~ DHYANI YWAHOO, NATIVE AMERICAN AUTHOR

WHEN I THINK ABOUT male rites of passage or even retreats that are planned
by men for men, I always think of them in a cabin, chopping wood, roast-
ing a pig that they've butchered, and going "back to the earth" in all ways
possible. Perhaps that's not everyone's picture, but many men I know like
to go "back to the earth," to sweat, to camp, to do activities traditionally
frontier-like and "manly."

I think, though, that going "back to earth" is not just manly, but en-
tirely human. Perhaps I'm connected with this idea because I like to chop

wood, sweat, and camp, but I don't think that's the only reason. Certainly each person is drawn to different activities, but we were drawn from the earth, from dust. The Genesis 2 account makes our origin the earth, though we have the breath of God. Humans were created to be connected to the earth—to physical creation.

Our Bodies = Every Body

Whether we know ourselves to be connected to the earth or not, we do know ourselves as connected to our earthly bodies. In the section on relationship with self we explored the connection between body and soul and how physicality and spirituality intertwine. We have sought to understand our bodies by charting our cycles and agreeing with what our bodies reveal to us rather than fighting with them.

When God called humans "very good," God was not only referring to our souls, but also to our bodies. Our heavenly future consists of a glorified *body*, a banqueting table, and a new heaven and new earth—these images are not simply spiritual, but incorporate physicality. When Christ became human, he sanctified the physical body even further than God's declaration of "very good." God not only looked on the outside and declared goodness, but God also inhabited the human body—an unfathomable mystery, the contemplation of which brings joy.

Our physical bodies can feel pleasure—even if it's in the creaminess of Lindt chocolate, the accomplishment of a physical feat, or the connectedness with another human in sexual intercourse. Our bodies can also feel pain—the pain of an upset stomach, a deep injury or disease, or even the pain of great physical distance between us and loved ones. Our senses are good and allow us to experience much—of one another, of creation, of sight, sound, taste, touch, and smell.[1]

It's not just our body, but every body. And let's simply begin with human bodies. We care for our bodies, yes, but humans are interconnected, and we are called to care for every body. God called us "very good," so how can we ignore others in the image of God that are also "very good"? When I buy a blood diamond, I care only for my body, but not for the bodies of those who are destroyed by working in that industry. When I buy from a corporation that has bought out local farmers, I do not care for the bodies

1. McMinn, *The Contented Soul*, 129–30.

of those farmers who have moved into the cities and are working in sweat-shops.[2] Bodies are sacred. Every body.

Exploring our world through hiking, history, and travel connects us with others who have gone before us. As a child, I loved visiting Mesa Verde National Park in the southwest corner of Colorado. I would gaze into the twelfth-century ruins carved into the cliffs and imagine what life must have been like for those living at the time. I've always felt somehow connected to and interested in the bodies of that time period.

I like to think I care about other bodies in the world, but I don't always. I think I'm pretty good—I recycle, I walk to work, I eat little meat, but when I assess my ecological footprint, it states that if everyone lived like me, we would need 2.2 planet earths to support our lifestyle. In other words, it is impossible for everyone to live like me and survive. The fact that I live the way I do may not feel like it directly causes suffering to other bodies in the world, like the starving children I see in documentaries, but it does. I am not caring for those bodies because of my excess and care only for my own. "Considering only the well-being of my own soul leads to emptiness . . . . [Perhaps we can] see ourselves as people who belong to God, to others, and to the earth from which we come."[3] It's not just our body, it's every body.

Loving God = Loving Creation

> As Christians living in the West, some of us have tended to believe that the earth is a temporary home that will one day pass away. Since saving souls has mattered more than saving matter (whether human, whale or tree), we've justified using this way station called earth however we've seen fit so long as we're working on saving souls . . . . This separation of the spiritual from the physical has meant that we've sometimes pitted caring for creation against caring for people. Caring for people has been a high priority for the church. *But in the twenty-first century we can't adequately care for people without giving some good attention to caring for the earth.*[4]

Saving souls is a wonderful priority, but we cannot save souls if we do not care for bodies. And caring for bodies entails caring for the earth that nourishes our bodies. "At our point in history loving others depends on

2. Ibid., 131.

3. Ibid., 139.

4. McMinn and Neff, *Walking Gently on the Earth*, 17; emphasis original.

our attending to creation because people's well-being depends on a healthy planet. Loving others may require us to take and use no more than we need, and to do so in ways that do not harm what others need to flourish."[5]

I remember in my seminary theology class that one of my favorite professors, Dr. Siu, stated that he loved the church. He said that he wanted to love what God loved and God loved the church, so Dr. Siu also loved the church. I found his thoughts inspiring. Because I did not always love the church at that point in my life, I prayed that the Lord would give me a love for the church because I wanted to love what God loved.

My love for the church grew.

Perhaps, like Dr. Siu I could stand in front of a classroom and say, "I love the world. All the creatures and all living, growing things of the world—I love it all. I want to love what God loves and God clearly loves the world."

God established a covenant not just with Noah, but also with all creatures on the earth. God said to Noah that the covenant was "with every living creature that was with you—the birds, the livestock and all the wild animals, all those that came out of the ark with you—every living creature on earth. I establish my covenant with you: Never again will all life be destroyed by the waters of the flood; never again will there be a flood to destroy the earth" (Gen 9:9–11). God covenanted with humans *and* with creatures.

When the Lord speaks at the end of Job, chapters 38–41, it is clear that God is intimately involved with all creation. In rhetorical questions, God asks Job if he has been involved in the movements of the animals, the stars, and the sun, as God has. Job realizes that God is involved in all creation, and is completely humbled. God is profoundly active in all creation, and creation—creatures, rocks, trees—is valuable because God gives it value.[6]

Furthermore, all creatures, whether they are animate or inanimate, worship God.[7] Revelation declares that all creatures "in heaven and earth and under the earth and on the sea and all that is in them" praise God (Rev 5:13). Jesus does not rebuke his disciples for praising him, for even the rocks will cry out if they don't (Luke 19:40), and Paul states that all creation "has been groaning in labor pains until now; and not only the creation, but we ourselves, who have the first fruits of the Spirit, groan inwardly while

5. Ibid., 23.

6. Ibid., 20

7. Bauckham, "Stewardship and Relationship," 104.

we wait for adoption, the redemption of our bodies" (Romans 8:22–23, NRSV). Somehow, creation understands and looks forward to what God will do. Finally, the Psalmist sings,

> The heavens declare the glory of God;
>   the skies proclaim the work of his hands.
>
> Day after day they pour forth speech;
>   night after night they reveal knowledge (Ps 19:1–2).

Creation has value because God has given it value, and it worships God.

And when Jesus speaks of the birds in the Sermon on the Mount, he is encouraging us not to worry. What we don't always notice (since we tend to focus on God's care for ourselves) is that God cares for the smallest birds and the flowers of the field.

> Look at the birds of the air; they do not sow or reap or store away in barns, and yet your heavenly Father feeds them. Are you not much more valuable than they? . . . And why do you worry about clothes? See how the flowers of the field grow. They do not labor or spin. Yet I tell you that not even Solomon in all his splendor was dressed like one of these. If that is how God clothes the grass of the field, which is here today and tomorrow is thrown into the fire, will he not much more clothe you—you of little faith? (Matt 6:26, 28–30)

Yes, God cares for *us* and calls us not to worry, but God also cares for the birds. God feeds the birds and clothes the grass of the field. Furthermore, God knows when a sparrow, a cheap commodity at the time of Jesus, dies. "Are not two sparrows sold for a penny? Yet not one of them will fall to the ground outside your Father's care" (Matt 10:29).[8] God cares enough for the sparrows to understand their lives. God loves not only the creatures of the ground and air, but also the grass of the field. I want to love what God loves. As one who bears the image of God, I can.

"This is God's earth and he commands us to be good stewards of it, a truth which often goes unseen and is forgotten."

We Westerners have an interesting relationship with ownership—we want to own it all, and sometimes we think and act like we actually do. Our attitudes show that not only do our bookbag, body, and car belong to us, but so

---

8. The context of this passage, again, is Jesus encouraging others not to be afraid.

does the land, if we purchase property. And even if it doesn't, we may treat it rather worse than we would our own yard—as evidenced by the litter I find every time I hike. Often, we litter and destroy what belongs to others more than we would litter what belongs to us.

We take down forests because they are ours, and often do not replenish the land. We build cities in the desert and then water their grassy lawns by depleting aquifers, all for the sake of the "American Dream." Our developments crowd animals out of their habitats, causing them to invade others', but it doesn't matter because they are off our property. If it's mine I get to do what I want with it, no?

Native Americans saw the earth quite differently. They had no thoughts of owning the earth, but believed they belonged to the land. The land, in a sense, was greater than they. "We are not used to thinking of ourselves as belonging to the earth or being obligated to others with whom we share it."[9] Perhaps, as we think of our bodies as well as every body, our understanding of the earth could move from being only ours to being everybody's. We all depend on the earth.

> "We are part of creation and are responsible for its conservation. It takes time and discipline to steward creation but it is a blessing to do so."

I remember being in Syria in May of 2012, and seeing the fruit and vegetable vendors as I walked down the street. When I first arrived, they had fuzzy green crescent-shaped unripened almonds and round green plums. I tried an almond once, and the plums were always available at Amal's house. We would dip them in salt and crunch away as we puckered at their sourness.

Throughout the next few months, different fruits progressively filled the vendors' carts, each for but a short time. The strawberries were the best I've ever tasted, and we made strawberry jam. The cherries and melons were delectable, and as we walked home, we would eat a dozen juicy apricots each. I was surprised to see Amal boiling a huge vat of peas one afternoon. But she only partially boiled them, placing them in Ziplocs after they cooled, and putting them in the freezer in the basement. She did the same for the huge artichoke hearts, and so did everyone. Springtime and into summer was the time to gather all the great fruit and vegetables, eat, and then can and freeze them, in order to bring them out in the middle of

9. McMinn, *The Contented Soul*, 132.

winter when spring seemed so far away. The excitement of the first crop of apricots was palpable—the people loved being so connected to the land.

We, too, can connect ourselves to the land and to each other. It is a process, especially for Westerners, to connect ourselves in that way, but we can only buy fruit and vegetables that are in season, or only those that are local. We can recycle, walk to work, and cut down on our meat consumption. We can make ourselves aware of our ecological footprint and take steps to make it smaller. Though it may be a long, hard process, we can begin.

When I read McMinn and Neff's *Walking Gently on the Earth*, I wrote on one of the first pages, "I want to be a person who thinks globally, but acts locally like this. In doing so, I want to think daily about *all* life in this world—to honor Indonesia by a short shower," and there I stopped. I'm not sure if it was because I knew that taking short showers would be very difficult for me, or because I had no other ideas. In Indonesia, we took bucket showers because of the shortage of water. In Syria, during the dry winter months, they only have running water for a few hours daily, so they store it in tanks. Showers need to be short there, too. I love my long, hot showers. Can I give them up or at least shorten them bit by bit because I have a relational obligation to others in the world, and how I use my resources is not just about me? I hope so. I want to love what God loves not just in my head, but also with my actions.

Perhaps I could see the earth as God does. Perhaps I could go for a walk and hear the early birds' song as a melody that worships their God with joy and exuberance. I could look at the colors of a flower or tree and be amazed at the radiance reflected back at me in the intricacy. I could see the rivers and waterfalls as that which is bound in and let loose by God for beauty and for service to the rest of creation. Perhaps I could be like a little girl who exults in watching and chasing butterflies—every day, because she never gets bored of them, loving what God loves and seeing the beauty.

To chat about over tea, coffee, and/or chocolate:

Do you agree that we are called to care for creation? Why or why not?

What do you hope your part will be in conservation? How do you plan to move forward in this area?

Prayer

Almighty and most gracious God, I praise you for your creation is fearful and wonderful. I also declare that you are the trustworthy God who is always worthy of my actions and attitude of trust. Teach me to be a Sabbath-honorer and a conserver of creation. Transform my heart to understand how I am a creature in the midst of creation. I want to live to praise you. In the name of the Father, the Son, and the Holy Spirit, One God, forever and ever.

Amen.

16

To Fashion and Form

Creativity

Everybody born comes from the Creator trailing wisps of glory. We come from the Creator with creativity. I think that each one of us is born with creativity.

~ MAYA ANGELOU

Creativity taks courage.

~ HENRI MATISSE, FRENCH ARTIST

All I can say is, hey, if you have fun doing what you do, if you have fun playing soccer, the creativity is just going to come as time goes on.

~ FREDDY ADU, GHANA-BORN AMERICAN SOCCER PLAYER

NOT ONLY DO I want to love what God loves, but I also want to do what God does, in the best way that a fallen human created in God's image can. God created, and as those in God's image, we are also those who create. We never create something out of nothing, as God did, but we can take what is already there, and create with it. We humans are inherently creative.

As you read this, some of you may be inspired to realize that your creativity is actually part of your relationship to creation; you may be excited to embark on creative tasks as one in the image of God! Others of you may not yet consider yourselves creative; in fact, you may have always wished to be creative, but in your final judgment, you are sorely lacking. I hope the thoughts that follow might serve as inspiration for your creativity, though your creative expression may differ from what is conventionally defined as creative.

A Creative Definition

Writer Vinita Hampton Wright suggests that we are *all* creative. Her work seeks to connect spirituality and creativity and to inspire creative writing. She states,

> In a general sense, every human being is creative. This trait is not always flashy. Often it's not called by its true name. But when you take the stuff of life and rearrange it so that it matters, so that is does good things, you're acting creatively. At those times when you are breaking a sweat to make life work better, you are most like the God who created you. You don't have to come up with a new idea in order to be creative. All you have to do is find an old idea and apply it to a new moment or group of people, a new problem or situation.[1]

Professor Howard G. Hendricks adds that creativity is for the benefit of others, and is often simply perceiving in a way not everyone perceives.[2]

I invite you to take a moment and ponder these assertions, especially if you're not sure you're all that creative. Do you ever take the stuff of life and rearrange it so it works and matters? Do you rearrange in what we would call a creative way, like rearranging words on a page in writing poetry or prose, words in the air in drama and lyrics, colors on a page or computer screen in visual art or graphic design, the pieces of stone or clay to form an image, or even your body in dance or athletics? When you spend days and hours moving your body to complete the perfect triple axel, the best shot at the goal, or the perfect lay-up, you are "rearranging" your body so it works well.

Creativity is not limited to visual art, but also encompasses architecture, engineering, and even science, for we create experiments. Though some types of creativity feel life-giving to us and others feel more like

1. Wright, *The Soul Tells a Story*, 17.
2. Hendricks, *Color Outside the Lines*, 23.

work, even rearranging the thoughts of others and using them to prove a point in a research paper is creative. Making jewelry from beads and doing something "different" when you lead a meeting is creative. Some of us show our creativity in the way we dress and use makeup, or through body art. Though it is variously expressed, sometimes "flashily" and sometimes not, we are all creative.

When I teach on creation in my Christian thought class, I give the students Play-Doh. And they love it. We talk about being in the image of God, and how that makes us creative, and they listen and create with their hands at the same time. Whether they make a Play-Doh snowman or a car, their smiles parallel any small child's, because creativity brings joy to our souls.

Howard Hendricks encourages creative leadership. He writes that we all have significant creative potential, but that *"conditioning is often fatal to the creative process.* One of the main reasons so many people seem to lack creativity is that the creative sparks they actually do possess have been doused by years of negative conditioning."[3] Whether someone has been told they are not creative, or their creative ideas have been rejected, people often move away from creativity to follow the conventional "rules" of society and the workplace, rather than joyfully being creative in those same places.

I find creativity to be vulnerable. I remember the hours I spent writing my dissertation on rites of passage for women. It was months of what felt like blood and sweat, and was literally accompanied by the shedding of tears. Though it was research, it was deeply creative, even if it felt more creative in a dry, academic sense than anything else. At the point, however, when I was first to present it to others, I was indescribably nervous. I did not sleep the night before, and I felt vulnerable, deeply vulnerable. Because I had spent so much time and effort in this area and believed in it deeply, it felt like I was presenting *myself*, not simply my research, and opening myself up to public shaming should it not be received. My creativity is an extension of myself, and it makes me feel vulnerable.

I have since gotten beyond some of thay anxiety and vulnerability, but I still find that in the areas that are most important to me and in those where I am forming something new, I feel most intimidated. I am at my most creative, but I sometimes procrastinate (not my preferred mode) because it feels vulnerable. Creativity is risky.

3. Ibid., 3–5; emphasis original.

Alice Bass, author of *The Creative Life: A Workbook for Unearthing the Christian Imagination,* asserts that because we are in the image of the creative God, faith and creativity are necessarily intertwined. "To enjoy a creative life we need to be free to experience more of Christ's inspiration and less of our own inhibitions, fears, and sin patterns."[4] It's like she was reading my journal, no? If we pay less attention to our own inhibitions and fears, we can truly insert ourselves into a life of creativity that grows out of our life in Christ, sharing one image. She adds that we are naturally (or shall we say creationally) imaginative, and imagination is part of creativity.[5]

Singer-songwriter Michael Card asserts that creativity is worship, since it is a response to God.[6] All of our worship responds to who God is and what God does; creativity is a response to who God is *in us*, and what God does *in us*. Our creativity is not separate from God's image, rather it is part of God's image, intertwined beautifully with faith and spirituality while opposing inhibitions and fears.

A Creative Life

I participated in many outdoor activities as a young girl, but I found that my brother explored the world in a way that was different from me. He not only dressed up in camouflage for "war" with his friends or simply to scare my friends and me, but he also went through a time of deep interest in survival skills. This was, of course, long before we watched people trying to use such skills in reality shows. We had plenty of fallen trees in the woods, and Brian had learned how to make a shelter in the woods out of branches and sticks beside a fallen tree. He showed it to us and though it looked small to me, he (almost) spent one night in it. If I recall correctly, he did not make it the whole night, but he still loved this manner of showing creativity.

We will all show creativity in different ways, but when I read that creativity is exploratory[7] and an adventure,[8] I thought of my brother. He explored the world around him, and honestly, it made him different from a lot of other kids, but no matter. He knew who he was and what he was interested in. Today, he dabbles in welding bike frames together to create newer

4. Bass, *The Creative Life,* 17.

5. Ibid., 20.

6. Card, *Scribbling in the Sand,* 29.

7. Wright, *The Soul Tells a Story,* 19.

8. Hendricks, *Color Outside the Lines,* 7.

shapes with wheels to take him places, and enjoys physics experiments with the students he teaches. For him, it is all an adventure.

Not everyone understands creativity, and people may wonder why my brother didn't just get a tent, buy an expensive bike frame, or go with the tried and true experiments. But creativity explores, asks questions, adventures, and sometimes makes others uncomfortable.[9]

"This [adventure] is key. To be most effective, creativity must pervade all of life—from writing letters to wrapping Christmas presents, from preparing meals to making love. It does not exist in isolation. It is not suddenly turned on . . . . Creativity affects one's thinking, behavior, attitudes, values, and communication."[10] Creativity is not something we place in a safe box and take out here and there, but it engages all of who we are—emotionally, intellectually, spiritually, physically, etc. We cannot compartmentalize it, for once we unleash creativity, it begins to beautifully flow throughout all of who we are as well as out from us. When I think of powerful art— whether it's a beautiful sunset over the Grand Canyon, Judy Chicago's *The Dinner Party* at the Brooklyn Museum, an expressive photo of a character-wrinkled face, a song sung from the depths of one's being, or a dance that takes me to another world—tears come to my eyes. The art engages me, not only visually, but viscerally—emotionally, intellectually, spiritually, and more—not just with my outward senses, but with all the sensibilities I have. Others' creativity engages me completely,[11] as does my own. When I engage in an activity and hours pass unnoticed, I am working from my creative core.

Cultivating Creativity

We are formed for a life of creativity, however that may be expressed in each person, but it takes cultivation and practice. If you've had your creative flames "doused," it takes a new perspective to move forward into creativity. Finding one's "creative niche" takes time, exploration, and desire.

Even the most basic activities can be creative. One friend of mine loves to prepare the table for the meals she hosts, and her table always looks incredible. In addition to painting, she takes her time and thinks a lot when decorating the areas of her home. She waits until she finds just the right

9. Wright, *The Soul Tells a Story,* 19.

10. Hendricks, *Color Outside the Lines,* 7.

11. Ibid., 21.

item for the wall, the desk, or the corner, and relishes the "fit" when it's all put together. Creativity is not in a rush.

Another friend has made cooking an act of creativity. She seeks to make each meal as colorful as possible, and as she chops and steams, she enjoys working with her hands and bringing bounty to her table. I enjoy cooking for a similar reason—it strengthens my relationship to creation when I create with the fruit of the earth, and working with my hands refreshes me from working with my mind all day.

My mother gardens. Though there's not much sun in the tree-filled backyard, there's a large garden of shade plants. My mother likes to feel the warm sun on her neck as she weeds and nourishes plants she brought from her beloved father's garden. She also places rocks and other decorations carefully to adorn the area and make it beautiful. Creativity can be expressed in a variety of ways.

Wright states, "Creativity may involve an artistic temperament—and it may not."[12] This is a good reminder. She suggests several actions to nurture creativity, including looking back for clues as to your preferred areas of creativity, following your joy, talking to your friends about your preferred area of creativity, and taking note of others' responses to your work.[13] These actions are instrumental in following the creative path.

All in all, however, creativity does not need to be complex, but is part of our everyday lives. Alice Bass reminds us, "God is around us, above us and in us. When we explore our creativity in him, he is not shocked by our huge ideas. Our giant dreams shatter only our own puny agendas and the glass minds of those around us."[14] Allow yourself freedom to dream and explore your creativity within God's limitless creativity, not hemmed in by your own fears and limiting of yourself. You are free to move forward and live a creative life.

> Oh, the depth of the riches of the wisdom and knowledge of God!
> How unsearchable his judgments,
> and his paths beyond tracing out!
> "Who has known the mind of the Lord?
> Or who has been his counselor?"

12. Wright, *The Soul Tells a Story*, 22.
13. Ibid., 24.
14. Bass, *The Creative Life*, 38.

"Who has ever given to God,
that God should repay them?"
For from him and through him and for him are all things.
To him be the glory forever! Amen (Rom 11:33–36).

I'm not sure why, but more than any other section in this book, I want to
break forth into song, as Paul did, as I complete this one on creativity. Perhaps it's because in writing about relationship to creation, I feel enlivened to
my core, and inspired to connect with all I see around me. I feel an organic
sense of joy and completion.

I hope that sense is one we share on this journey of Sabbathing,
conserving, and creating. Though I rejoice in completion, I also enjoy the
process we can experience as we move forward in our relationship to creation. The sharing of Sabbath rest is something I long for. In a culture that
is against this rest, I have long desired a community that rests in God's completion together and seeks to practically trust God in this way. And when I
put out my recycling, endeavoring to also reduce and reuse in the house, I
would love to peer down the street and see my neighbors all doing it, too.
Sharing the fruit of the earth in a community garden is another dream. I
also hope to look at others' creativity as beautiful, and not as a rival to my
personal creativity. Each one's creative image is different, offering differing
gifts to the world. May we be those who move forward in all these areas!

To chat about over tea, coffee, and/or chocolate:

Tell me about your creativity.

How do you hope to express more creativity in the future?

How do you now understand your relationship with creation?

Prayer

Almighty and most gracious God, I praise you for your creation is fearful
and wonderful. I also declare that you are the trustworthy God who is always worthy of my actions and attitude of trust. Teach me to be a Sabbath-
honorer and a conserver of creation. Transform my heart to understand the
creativity you have placed in me and how I am a creature in the midst of

creation. I want to live to praise you. In the name of the Father, the Son, and the Holy Spirit, One God, forever and ever.

Amen.

17

Where Do We Go From Here?

Conclusion

And so we still have a long, long way to go before we reach the promised land of freedom. Yes, we have left the dusty soils of Egypt, and we have crossed a Red Sea that had for years been hardened by a long and piercing winter of massive resistance, but before we reach the majestic shores of the promised land, there will still be gigantic mountains of opposition ahead and prodigious hilltops of injustice . . . Where do we go from here? First, we must massively assert our dignity and worth. We must stand up amid a system that still oppresses us and develop an unassailable and majestic sense of values. We must no longer be ashamed of being black.

~ MARTIN LUTHER KING JR., "WHERE DO
WE GO FROM HERE?"

I am a woman in process. I'm just trying like everybody else. I try to take every conflict, every experience, and learn from it. Life is never dull.

~ OPRAH WINFREY

MAY I WRITE YOU a letter? The kind that I always want to receive? The kind that I'd like to write to every spiritual daughter I've ever had?

A letter that would be dog-eared as the years go by because you keep bringing it out to remind you that *you can do this*?

A letter infused with love and encouragement that reminds you of reality and still brings you to hope?

An epistle that grounds you, but still calls you forward?

May I?

July 8, 2014

My Dear, Dear Woman,

You've made it! And I am so proud of you! You have walked through the challenges in these pages and been transformed. As I've shared my story and you've shared yours, we've journeyed together intensely. I will miss this time of intensity, but we knew it was only for a time. You are moving on, and I am staying here for now.

Please know that I will always be here. Here for you. Even if it's been years since we last connected, and I've connected with so many others, I still remember you. I still remember sharing this journey. Don't be afraid to ask me or the others who journeyed with you for help. We actually like to help you.

Remember that habit? It was one of four life habits that we developed together—naming ourselves "woman," asking for help, investing in ourselves, and embracing our own unique journey. I hope that wherever you are now, you will practice these. Please know that if you're in a vocation that you love by your early thirties, you're doing so much better than most, so choose daily to embrace your journey!

The path that you are walking has been ordained by the God who births like a mother. God even births dreams in you! The Psalmist cries to God,

> For you created my inmost being;
> you knit me together in my mother's womb.
> I praise you because I am fearfully and wonderfully made;
> your works are wonderful, I know that full well.
> My frame was not hidden from you when I was made in the secret place,
> when I was woven together in the depths of the earth.
> Your eyes saw my unformed body;
> all the days ordained for me were written in your book before one of them came to be.
> How precious to me are your thoughts, God!

How vast is the sum of them!

Were I to count them, they would outnumber the grains of sand—

when I awake, I am still with you (Ps 139:13–18).

God is with you at all times, creating your path.

God has made you and called you very good, including even those feminine characteristics that the world puts down. You are formed in the image of God—to be in relationship and to steward the world around you. Take both seriously—relationship and stewardship.

And remember the examples of those who've gone before—the women you know, and the women about whom you only read—Mary, Deborah, Huldah, Martha, Priscilla, Phoebe, and more! Although your journey is your own, it may look similar to theirs at times, so be encouraged and emboldened! Your emotions and femaleness are *good* and Godlike.

Continue to develop your relationship with God, for like all real relationships, it takes work. In fact, I've found that when I'm in the "real world" and not in a more focused environment like college or a group of women, relationships take more work than I could possibly imagine. Expect setbacks since life happens; don't give up but diligently pursue relationships that matter!

And don't forget yourself. Never forget yourself—you are important, though sometimes you feel like you're the only one who remembers. Believe it or not, you aren't the same person you were last year or the same person you will be next year. Take time to know yourself through the joyful and painful seasons by spending time alone in reflection; take time to embrace the changes on the journey and to fully experience them. Fight bitterness with all that is in you through embracing your unique life.

Your menstrual cycle may change for various reasons; your body may begin to look better or worse to you; pregnancy, childbirth, or menopause can change everything. Remember that the goal is health, not a particular size, so exercise and eat well, choosing to bless your body rather than curse it. Choose always to bless, even when you don't feel like it. Also, adorn your body in a way that makes you feel good.

And give life—give life to your children, to nieces and nephews, to friends, to gardens, to projects. . . . You are uniquely created to give life! And it is obvious that the world around us needs that life.

Allow the way you treat yourself to boost your confidence and voice. You have a voice that brings life to the world, and when you don't use it, everyone misses out. Use it, and use it with confidence, no matter how fast your heart beats or how your hands sweat when you speak. As you get used to using your voice, your heartbeat will become normal and your hands less clammy. Don't be afraid, but be strong and courageous.

Strength and courage often come through surrounding yourself with fantastic people—peers, mentors, and friends—both male and female. When you know yourself and bring her to others and follow Jesus' example in relationships, others can encourage, correct, and enjoy life with you along the journey. Some relationships are for a season and some for a lifetime, so let seasonal friends go, but hang on tight to the lifetime ones. Choose whose voices you will heed while discarding others you don't trust.

Be careful—not all can be trusted. Be care-full—full of caring words, actions, and love.

And date. Have fun with it; be serious when it's time. Do it well, with respect for him and yourself.

Your relationships with God, self, and others are just as important as your relationship with creation; you've just been previously taught it's less. All of these relationships affect one another and continuing to develop *all four* will be best for your life.

So, embrace the rest of God. Sabbath as best you can and invite others to do it with you. Take care, not only of the humans that surround you, but also of creation, knowing that in the end that's also caring for other humans, other bodies.

And as a woman formed in the image of God, create. Create what is good and right with the creativity inherent in your nature. Splash colors on your canvas or words on your pages or do whatever creativity fits you best. Do it with abandon, with joy, with your heart.

Enjoy your life. Recently I was thinking about the fact that we use the word *enjoy* to denote simply "having," as in, "residents will enjoy the pool on the property." The truth is, many residents will never use the pool, but will always have access to it. Think about enjoyment as having and using well. Enjoy your life, simply because you have it.

Enjoy it, embrace it. Embrace your relationships with God, others, self, and creation. Embrace who you are and who you are becoming. Embrace your womanhood. Take all of it up in your arms in an exuberant, encompassing hug, for this life is yours. These relationships are yours. The choices are yours.

And you are very good. For God created you very good and is restoring the divine image in you daily through the redeeming power of Jesus. Choose to dwell on this truth.

The journey that you are on, though it may not be easy, is still a good one. Hope in the Lord.

> Even youths grow tired and weary, and young men stumble and fall;
> but those who hope in the Lord will renew their strength.
> They will soar on wings like eagles;
> they will run and not grow weary, they will walk and not be faint
> (Isa 40:30–31).

I remember Tim Keller preaching on this once—he said that there was a reason for the order—soaring, running, walking. We want to soar, but life does not always feel like we're soaring; we want to run without weariness, but that's not always the case, either. We can always walk. And that's the point, walking.

So, walk this journey of womanhood well, my friend, my sister. Do it with gusto, and know that I'm cheering for you, as are so many others.

I am for you.

I am proud of you.

With Love,

Amy